ALL ROADS LEAD TO YOU

(NOT ANOTHER BLOODY SELF HELP)

LE FEEBS

Le Feebs Limited
United Kingdom

ALL ROADS LEAD TO YOU

(NOT ANOTHER BLOODY SELF-HELP)

Published by Le Feebs 2014
For more information visit: www.lefeebs.com

Cover photo by: Le Feebs
Cover design by: Le Feebs
Web photo: Palak Bhatt

Editor: Adam's Abundance Limited
Printed in the United Kingdom
ISBN-13: 978-0-993-07680-0
ISBN-10: 0-993-07680-7

Presented to:

From:

To my parents, without your union I wouldn't be here.

To my mother, you are my spine, my soul mate, my Automated Teller Machine and my biggest fan. You are blessed.

To my gorgeous niece Fien and my wonderful godson Nathaniel, I love you both to infinity and beyond.

To the cycles of existence, thank you for strengthening me with your lows and using them to propel me to higher highs.

To the school of the charmed life, continue to keep it easy, fun, adventurous, playful, challenging, exciting and fresh,

To my Higher Self, without you I will definitely still be asleep, though who's to say that I'm actually awake. HA!

Contents

The Journey to Me

On the happy and joyous journey to me I discover I am god. The power to do whatever I want is within me. Nobody can stop me. I am an eternal, limitless being. The limits I experience are those I choose to impose on myself. The gods I experience are ones that I choose to believe in and give power to.

On the fruitful and blissful journey to me I am god and god is I. I am the "I AM". We are everything and we are everywhere. We are, all knowing, all powerful and all seeing. I AM always growing and expanding because new experiences and unchartered territories befall me. I AM GOD!

On the prolific and euphoric journey to me the two intertwine and function as one. By choosing this domain I undermine myself as The Creator for a time. Before I was, I chose my entity, therefore my purpose is whatever purpose I give myself, my mission in life is the mission I choose for myself. I am tomorrow whatever I love to do today.

On the abundant and plentiful journey to me, nature is ample and infinite, as only oceans of bounty flow through me.

Le Feebs

PREFACE

Most books have a compelling narrative behind it. In my case, the thought of writing a book felt inappropriate and comical to me. I'd heard of the old adage that everyone had a book in them, but I positively didn't think mine would show up so soon. Surely I hadn't lived and experienced enough to feel so entitled and knowledgeable? In my very limited thought framework, a far richer and convincing story was needed to induct me into the writing hall of fame. I was hesitant to put thoughts to paper because in my view, knowledge and wisdom are infinite.

Rumour has it that as humans we change every seven years and I was on the cusp of adulthood where my faculties of insight, intuition, discernment and understanding were coming to the fore. I wanted to make sure that when I looked back in seven years the fundamental concepts in this book will not have changed for me. Honestly, the minute you think you've got it all figured out and mastered, something comes along to feed you humble pie.

It finally hit me that this book was a product of the season and cycle of life I was in. It was time to grow up and take full responsibility for my life and this was a necessary consolidating, crystallising and cathartic way to be initiated into adulthood. The more I uncovered, the more I unveiled the depth of my ignorance and it was not a pretty sight. Nevertheless, I stayed open to Creation and came to understand that writing was important as it freed the mind and freed the acquisition of knowledge.

Backpacking in Australia, bungee jumping in New Zealand, falling in love with a blonde-haired, blue-eyed Adonis and participating in a flash mob was the dream. I certainly did not anticipate this manuscript so early on in life. Little did I know that I was already on a journey, an adventure of sorts, specifically, one of self-awareness. I'm defining '**self-awareness**' here as the point where you realise the truth of who you really are and the part you play in humanity from broader perspective.

The impulse to start writing was not explicitly inspired by anyone, but rather through a series of prompts via synchronicities, events, close friends, acquaintances, God, Prime Creator or whatever name one gives the higher subtle force that permeates through all electrons, neutrons, atoms, molecules, ions and matter.

Understandably some may not take to the contents of this book, kindly note that it was not written with you in mind. The approach and the expression may reach only those who are exploring similar life themes or those who want to fund my Australian Odyssey (i.e. the obligatory friends and family purchase). At the very least, I'm optimistic that my narrative and perspective will speak to your heart as it's been written from the point of view of someone who's been there for the most part. What I lack in experience I hope I make up for, in wit and humour. Some words and concepts may offend as I only attempt to wake your sleeping consciousness.

Inspiration came from everywhere and new experiences energised me: my personal life, Facebook, Twitter, music, friends, acquaintances, films, family, books, conversations, pop culture and social interactions, you name it. The list is endless, and if it involved a life form or an activity; I learned something by observing it. Once, I popped into the supermarket to buy some provisions and parts of the book started forming in my head. Luckily I had my phone to hand to write some of it down. At times, I felt like the fictional character Dr. Gregory House in the House M.D. (TV series 2004-2012). In the middle of something I would suddenly have to stop and reach for my laptop or journal.

There were times I felt the physiological effects of tuning into new ways of thinking and being. This manifested itself in the form of a mild pulsatile tinnitus (hearing your blood flow in your ear drums) and some very strange dreams. Other times, I could only write about fifty words a day. There were times too where I completely disliked the book because my point of view changed daily based on new sensory data from all around. With no real end goal in mind, I enthusiastically went along with the concept of living my joy and if that joy involved sleeping, who was I to argue with the Universe? I've certainly learned to enjoy and appreciate the creative process. Probably the most important thing I learned on this metaphorical journey was to have no attachments to the outcome of this book. I was merely happy to be busy typing than watching paint dry. If it's a sure thing, why rush?

Life interrupted many times, as practicing the universal principles were paramount to my personal life, spiritual growth and the credibility of the book. I must admit, I lost my way several times, yet somehow I managed to find exactly where I was meant to be, because I used the golden nuggets in this book to overcome the emotional slumps and get my state of being back to a place of ease and pleasure. As I continued to write, I became increasingly convinced of the efficacy of the things you'll find described in this book because they all worked for me. There's absolutely nothing novel in here, just old ideas, remixed and expressed in a different way, my way. Ultimately the human experience is created primarily by the expression of beliefs, thoughts and the stories we tell ourselves.

FYI: I use God/Goddess/All That Is/Prime Radiant/Prime Creator/Creation/Higher Self/Source-Energy interchangeably throughout the book, as the force of life is genderless (both male and female in nature) and formless.

INTRODUCTION

"People take different roads seeking fulfilment and happiness. Just because they're not on your road doesn't mean they've gotten lost."

Dalai Lama XIV

Does the world need another book about the laws of the Universe?

Whilst writing, I often asked myself, what's the big idea? And does the world need another book concerning the laws of the Universe? The market was already flooded with many cult classics like 'Think and Grow Rich', 'The Power of Positive Thinking', 'Law of Success', 'The Secret', 'Ask and It Is Given' 'The Kybalion', 'The Master Key System' and many more. What was so different, unique and fresh about my perspective and were people going to be interested in what I had to say?

What was fresh about my approach was that it was inclusive, simple, honest and not one-dimensional. It trusted and empowered you to make all your decisions based on your preferences and nothing else, using the natural laws of life as your aide. For rather selfish reasons I also wrote it to remind myself how simple life can be if I just relaxed into it and worked with All That Is. In life, if you don't write your own story, someone else will write it for you and I was taking sole ownership of my narrative.

As a naturally inquisitive person I was never satisfied with the answers our leaders (politicians, scholars and people of that ilk) gave when posed difficult questions, hence I went searching for others. The big idea then, was to lay bare my findings from observations and personal experience and let you be the judge of what resonates and works for you. In addition, I was also tired of weird, freaky, mystic, new age quirks that alienated the masses from their knowledge and insights. I found life to be very simple, yet I realised others found joy in complicating it. The book title 'ALL ROADS LEAD TO YOU (NOT ANOTHER BLOODY SELF HELP)' was a foregone conclusion based on my big idea. There are many roads to self-awareness, once you understand the structure of the Universe, how it works and what drives us humans.

Throughout this book, I illustrate using metaphysical principles and anecdotes, to show that everyday life can be experienced in a peaceful and magical way, unless of course you prefer a more dramatic approach. Using some of the abstract concepts of metaphysics, I was able to better understand, navigate and transform my own personal challenges into ones of ease and triumph. I found that in life, you win even when you lose, because it's in the getting it wrong, that you possess the wherewithal to make it right.

It's by lightening up that you can have a taste of true enlightenment. One of my favourite quotes of all time is by Darryl Anka. He says, "*the greatest power requires the lightest touch*" and this statement rings true for me. Creation is the greatest power, yet it's hardly felt because it doesn't have to exercise its will or flaunt its power because it is EVERYTHING.

Coming up...

It's not an autobiography, although it might read like one and has a rhythmic flare to it. Portions of the book are dedicated to my poetry, observations, reflections and questions. The first chapter is a little summary of how I came to write 'ALL ROADS...' and the philosophical questions that eventually led me to think and act the way I do now. Chapter 2 is a summary of the events that lead me to my current spiritual path. Chapter 3 is closer look into metaphysics and some of the resulting theories. Chapter 4 tackles the infamous ego and my thoughts on it. In Chapter 5, I deal with transforming and redefining circumstances so they work for you in a wonderful way. Finally, Chapter 6 deals with limits, the nooks and crannies of why they exist and work for us.

DISCLAIMER: What you are about to delve into is both true and untrue, it is only by applying it will you find out (much like Schrodinger's cat). Everything expressed in this book at its core is merely an opinion. Take what you can from it and discard what doesn't work for you. The choice is completely yours as you have the free will and creative power to live as you see fit. If you're reading this, you're already through the looking glass anyway. Life experience is the best and most effective teacher hence; I trust that life will teach you what you need to know when you need to know it; not a moment before and not a moment after. Perchance, you might refer back to his book at some point in your life journey and remember that I told you first.

If you're sincere about taking full responsibility for your life, then let's examine the logic of the Universe together. Fingers crossed, it raises more answers than questions, which will lead to more questions.

WARNING! Don't be surprised if you suddenly realise you can do BETTER than the life you have settled for. Confidence and control triggers thoughts of upgrading. Take this momentum, embrace it below the surface and use it to your advantage.

CHAPTER ONE

DEFINING MOMENTS

"When you lose sight of your path, listen for the destination in your heart."

Katsura Hoshino

There is a plethora of defining moments in my life, but the most recent one was deciding to quit my job and go travelling. I'm very proud of myself for having the courage to walk away from things that no longer made me happy. After three years of working as a back office analyst in the financial services and some failed attempts at wanting to be a trader, I decided to quit my job on a whim. I learned at the outset that it wasn't an expression of my highest joy and passion because I didn't live and breathe finance and the macro economy. Back then, I couldn't give a rat's arse about what company was doing what with its IPO and how much money they had gained or lost in a day. Even when I psyched myself up with books like 'Reminiscences of a Stock Operator' by Edwin Lefevre and 'Lords of Finance' by Liaquat Ahamed there wasn't enough passion to manifest the trading dream. Although I passed the necessary exams to get onto the trading floor I always managed to sabotage my interviews. I developed some colorectal issues and I finally decided no amount of money, or debt could keep me in this sector because I wasn't happy and not for the lack of trying either. It was also that time to get off my derriere and invest in myself. For three years I recounted a story of deep hatred for my job and for my life choices. The unease I felt was my body's consciousness, screaming at me to listen to my heart and begin to narrate a story of vitality, joy, love and laughter.

This was an opportunity to really think about what I wanted and walking away seemed like the next logical step for me. As providence would have it, I had no major dependants and liabilities (bar lodgings and food). I was single, free and the timing was perfect for me. I decided that no matter what happened I would embrace it and use this period in my life as some form of an arbitrary reference point. From the outside looking in, I was making a mistake. In my heart I knew it was the dangling carrot and the 'umph' needed to make the triumphant shift into the next phase of my expedition. The only thing I knew without a shadow of a doubt was that I would get through this unscathed, smarter, happier, lighter, healed, wealthier and superconductive to all good things in the Universe. I wanted to be in a place where my lifestyle, funded my *lifestyle*. This was my ultimate fun-employed quest and I was crazy enough to actually believe it.

In retrospect, my fundamental beliefs and temperament were never suited to the fast paced, aggressive, dog-eat-dog, masked nature of the trading floor. I have no personal misgivings about the financial sector, as I owe it an enormous debt of gratitude for igniting the philosophical and entrepreneurial side of me and making it possible for me to follow my natural impulses. Their process of being and expressing was simply not my thing. In all honesty I always envisioned myself in a more relaxed, playful, fun, flexible, autonomous, unrestricted atmosphere with passions galore and I had no business in that reality.

In the long run, I reasoned that if I were being supported financially in something unwanted, how much more would life sustain me doing something that was an expression of my highest joy and purpose. They say you shouldn't expect to get 100% change in your physical reality if you only support it 50% and a job I wasn't particularly passionate about was not getting in the way of my 100% better reality.

This decision was to be my first conscious practical lesson in learning to identify my preferences and standing by them. Sometimes in life, to help define who you are and what you want, you have to experience the unwanted to clearly spell out your preferred reality. I was aware I needed a change, and so far I'd only worked out that I needed more ease, passion, fun and relaxation in my next experience. I had no real inkling of what my next career would look like or how to get there. We all have our individual quirks that make us who we are, and I wasn't quite sure what mine were because I was one of those annoying kids who could do everything in school if I put my mind to it. I was stuck in a place of lost and neglected things.

After some time, I took stock of what was available to me in the present and in terms of assets, I had a laptop, a fairly underused creative streak (painting, drawing, designing and writing), an overdraft, a credit card and tons of free time. For emotional support I had my old dear, some understanding friends, family and acquaintances. How was I going to transform these resources into something tangible, full of passion and excitement? This was another life lesson in learning to use the available resources to the best of my ability.

Initially I couldn't see what I could exchange my free time, limited credit and creativity for. It took several more months of solitude at the British Library, some botched attempts at meditation, a journal and drained resources for me to empty my head of dramatic expectations to finally sit down and do what came naturally to me. Unbeknownst to me, those aimless days were for gathering raw information and chewing it over in my system. I wrote the general themes of this book in three months and it took a further three months of editing and seamless behind the scenes events to get it to you.

It took me longer than necessary to start writing because my vivid imagination probably wanted to see angel wings, a burning bush, some flashing neon lights in Piccadilly Circus or something to that effect before I could make sense of my resources. Something film worthy at the very least, as this is my life we're talking about. My plan to also dream up some numbers and hit the Euro Millions Jackpot, retire and paint on a vineyard somewhere in Burgundy couldn't come soon enough.

I recognise now that a fun-employed quest might take you through deep seas; hikes, solitude, long strolls and bring it all back to focusing on you. You can never get it wrong no matter where you are, because it's in the getting it wrong that you are able to transform it into something better. My idle months cleared the mental space for me to see, hear and take action towards writing and building my own website. I got stuck in because the action brought me joy and purpose. Something I was lacking for a long time. They say, *"the road to success is never straight; there is a curve called failure, a loop called confusion, speed bumps called friends, red lights called contrast, caution lights called family. You will have flats called job, but if you have a spare called determination, an engine called perseverance, insurance called faith, a driver called God, you will make it to a place called success"*.

To give you some more context, it's Tuesday 22nd July 14, and I'm listening repeatedly to Little Wonders by Rob Thomas (Disney's Meet the Robinsons soundtrack) from the comfort of my bed, whilst reading the 'funniest texts between parents and their children ever sent' on lifebuzz.com. It is one of my favourite songs of all time alongside Coldplay's Don't Panic, for copyright reasons you'll have to Google the lyrics and find out why. It's midday and currently a steaming 19 degrees Celsius in London (yes 19 degrees is steaming). I'm gagging for a vanilla cream Frappuccino and a warm toasted fruit loaf with lashings of butter from Starbucks, but my overdraft is maxed out so a bottle of water and chilling in the bedroom it is. In addition, my mum has hinted several times to get a job (imagine the look of contempt on my face as she says the J word). In her defence I promised her I would have a job by July. My stress levels should be high but the heat coupled with my zero fucks attitude is keeping me fairly balanced. If Oscar Wilde taught me anything, it was that anyone living within their means showed a total lack of imagination. Things have not panned out the way I thought they would, and thank heavens they haven't. The best way I could handle it was by letting go and charging it to my life experience and soul education account.

For all intents and purposes I was under the illusion a job would materialise, but hey ho *whaddayaknow* it didn't. I spent a weekend completing some work for this 'so called job' and still naught. In life, it's imperative to invest wholeheartedly into anything, be it a job, a relationship (social or intimate) or a business and when you see no returns, walk away with your dignity and self-esteem intact. I find letting the laws of the Universe deal with whatever situation I'm in brings immediate relief and reassurance, as the natural laws deliver every time. That encounter was the Prime Creator's way of leading me back to focus whole-heartedly on my natural leanings and to always ask for a contract and/or an advance before expending any energy. Fortunately writing and admin for the book consumed my every waking moment and left me no room to feel sorry for myself.

Apart from the odd nostalgia about being able to afford things like a Starbucks and a falafel wrap with grated carrots (I hear they have been discontinued) from The Breakfast Club in Shoreditch, I maintain that quitting my job was the best decision I ever made and I have no regrets. The advantages of a 9-5 are that you're protected by your employee contract and guaranteed a monthly income. When you branch out on your own, you need your wits about you, coupled with unconditional trust in the benevolence of the Universe in order to thrive.

My voyage thus far has been anything but straightforward. With all the various curveballs thrown at me, I made a conscious decision early on to only engage in activities that excited me. My excitement took many forms, ranging from resting, reading, sketching, painting, dancing, puzzles and whatever other exciting thing my imagination conjured up moment-by-moment. By following my excitement, it made me curious about the world around me. For the first time in a long time, I could relax and enjoy life. I had no morning commute and everyone was pleasant on the 11.15am train to King's Cross Station. There was no one yelling 'MOVE INSIDE THE TRAIN PLEASE!' and I wasn't pushed up against someone's pits. I was open to everything and could learn from absolutely everyone. All that free time meant that I was now master of the Victoria Line and knew how to navigate Kings Cross and St. Pancreas station.

Excitement comes in many configurations and silhouettes. It's up to you to find out if something is truly exciting or whether it's being chosen out of anxiety rather than a place of integrity. If you limit your definition of fun to getting pissed and doing the walk of shame, you might wake up to a very shallow existence. When you broaden that definition to include simple things like enjoying a slice of toast, a distraction, or even a stroll, you'll be surprised at what life has in store for you. Every activity is injected with fun and enthusiasm. When you do what excites you, there are no other choices but to burn the bridges of boredom and dullness and face the fun challenges that come your way. Before you know it, your life becomes one exciting experience after another and people will wonder how you maintain a constant passionate state.

"In every job that must be done, there is an element of fun. You find the fun, and the job's a game." –P.L. Travers, Mary Poppins.

By following my excitement, I was being taught how to:

- Live in a constant creative energy field, spark curiosity and rediscover **PASSION**. The excitement trail eventually led me to a writing **PROJECT**.
- Get **PREPARED** and learn about the things relevant to my new project. Because I was passionate about life again, preparation was fun and easier than expected. There was only one rule, HAVE FUN!
- Interact with **PEOPLE**. I was talking to everyone about what I'd been up to for a whole year on my fun-employment quest. Naturally, people were also inquisitive about what I was up to because my life is just that interesting.
- To be **PERSISTENT**. I had to learn to continue with my course of action in spite of a dwindling savings account and popular opinion (you can never win in the court of public opinion).

Without meaning to I stumbled upon the **5 Ps**. The Universe through the use of subtlety and gentle nudges taught me the about the nuances of **passion**, **project**, **preparedness**, **people** and **persistence**. I was also learning to self-validate and be self-sufficient. It was my life and I was taking creative control.

Although I didn't have to quit my job to start being more present and appreciative of things around me, this was the way my story unfolded. I don't recommend my path because it is not for the faint-hearted. I understand the illusionary nature of life, so temporary reflections of lack and loss do not discourage me. I know beyond a shadow of a doubt that I am fully supported by All That Is in my excitement. So I can't make a few girls nights out, BOOHOO! I know where I belong and my decisions are representative of my intentions. I find that being flexible, open and adaptable helps you stay balanced and cheerful at all times because there is no pressure on the outcome. Everything that happens is exactly what is supposed to happen.

Defining moments then are really decision points in life about the life you prefer no matter how small or big they appear. It's a point where you are always choosing integration or segregation of your true self. The only action required in a defining moment is one of choice and everything else has no choice but to fall in place. As you stand in the midst of a reality you don't prefer, you clearly envision a reality you do prefer and you adjust your beliefs and align your actions to that of your new way of being. You inevitably attract an opportunity or circumstance that will reinforce the new defined YOU. And if things seem to be going haywire, there's always www.fmylife.com to give you the giggles about someone's life not panning out the way they planned too (**Law of Relativity** at its best).

Coming from a Christian background with some Muslim influences from my maternal grandfather's side, I could never explicitly say that one religion was better than the other. The thought of getting to heaven and leaving my loved ones behind was a hard pill to swallow. At a point in time, I decided to become a Muslim as well as a Jew. My religion was structured around fear, the fear of eternal damnation. My rationale was simply to have a huge chunk of the widely known monotheistic bases covered, and to ensure that if there was a hell, I had diversified and protected myself from going there (my enterprising nature always crept in). In my reformation days I also went to a Sikh temple with one of my girlfriends, but was not passionate enough about Punjabi to add it to my hell insurance policy.

My religious zeal tapered off at university, far away from my maternal influence in Scotland. Sundays became a day of recovery from nights out, instead of a Sunday morning service at church. All these reformations eventually took their toll and befuddled me. It appeared to me these monotheistic faiths were serving the same God but couldn't agree on the details of what he looked like and his personality. There were also too many rules and the whole set up became increasingly incompatible with my lifestyle.

In my opinion, religion can only be taken so far till it begins to prove counterproductive and I was daring enough to drop it. It's not so much that there's anything wrong with it, but when it starts to encroach on your human rights, development and leanings, I reckon it's time to let it go, unless you hold it as a crutch to be more of your natural self, in that case 'Kumbaya' all the way to the pulpit.

The Christian argument that I was born a sinner and had to make my way my back to heaven, no longer held any justification and credibility for me. I asked myself, why would God knowingly create me from the heavens, in his image and bring me to Earth with an outlaw's stamp on my forehead? Not only that, I had to repeatedly call the human form worthless, reject all carnal desires, work for absolution and chance my way into eternal life and a pie in the sky because you never actually knew when the overtly masculine God was going to strike you down as an insignificant being. I say chance, because after ensuring you followed the law to the letter, heaven was still not guaranteed. Not only was this version of God biased and gruesome, but he was also a jealous man with a seismic ego who only liked you if you liked his Son. Existing in this form damned me. I increasingly found this rendition of the God to be illogical and contradictory at its core.

To create something and put a negative label on it, then expect a good outcome from it after bombarding it with feelings of unworthiness sounded bizarre to me and went against the natural laws of life. I remember singing words like "though I'm not good enough, but he still loves me..." Over time, I realised that my understanding and interpretation of Christianity meant one could never measure up, no matter how good you were because ultimately you were born with the odds of a sinner.

I am inclined to think God is loving, genderless, colourless and formless. Sending a male heir as the only way to inner peace, perpetrating a fair image of him, as well as parading him as the only Lord and Saviour reeked of major ulterior motive. Such an image perpetuates racial division, gender tension and hubristic religious tendencies especially when we live in a multicultural, multi-racial, diverse world. You may chuckle, but a lot of countries, foundations, families, and businesses were founded on these principles, with women always being a little less than men across the board because they had no supreme being fighting their corner in recent history.

Unless you read the Apocrypha or other Gnostic versions of the Bible, it appears God only spoke through men too. Out of the sixty-six books in the bible only two books are named after women, Ruth and Esther with the authors unknown. Women have only 3% representation in the standard Bible, yet I see more women seeking validation en masse in that institution than men.

Women emulating men is widely accepted, but have men emulating women and witness the outrage. Men go as far as to insult themselves with female related words like pussy, bitch, soft, or even gay because anything less than the rustic male ego is considered lesser, powerless and futile. What's really funny about the whole thing is that women chime in too (the biggest cosmic joke ever). Now that is what I call successful conditioning.

Physiologically speaking, a woman's brain has more connections than a man, yet they can't be trusted to write or hear from God. We must submit to a man's authority because he is the head of the house, is physically stronger, knows better, is the main provider and how can I forget, the usual humdrum of women being too emotional. When the obvious contradictions are pointed out, you are met with 'the Bible is the Word of God' and they were right.

They were right on the premise that I was imposing my way of thinking and not allowing their path to be just as valid as mine. Truth is I was seeking pleasure in proving how wrong religion was and how right I was. I was reflecting the same ignorance I had waged a war against. I eventually understood that not everyone had to see things from my perspective because unconditional love allows for all to co-exist. When you know something, you don't need anyone else to jump on the same bandwagon. The truth needs no defence or allies. Those were the words of their God and I was clearly a mismatch. I no longer had dealings with this spiritual set up and it was time to get out of there with my sense making self. **Unconditional love here is being defined as love with NO CONDITIONS.** You are loved because you are loved. Whether you have done something terrible or not, love is never taken away from you. Instead your choices and underlying fears keep you away from the unconditional love of All That Is.

We are process-oriented beings. Everything we do as humans is to help us become more of our natural selves, be it religion, school, job, friends and relationships. Religion is a crutch that helps us believe that we are divine and wonderful and though our forms are suitable for earth our souls were just passing through. We recite mantras, quote scriptures, seek psychics, prophets and fortune-tellers to remind us of our worth and how loved we are. Through the process of education, we learn how to read, write, comprehend and make knowledge accessible. We use jobs as a process to provide, create value and express creativity and we use friendships and relationships to form bonds, build a picture of who we are and identify our shared values and preferred clusters. We also create enemies/opponents to act as catalysts to spur us on in the times of complacency. These processes in no shape or form define us, we give it meaning and render it relevant in our day-to-day lives.

These were merely some of the thought processes floating around on my journey of self-discovery. I don't for one minute doubt the existence of Jesus and the essence of what he still stands for; however, I believe his message has been redacted and contaminated over time by different political ideologies, hidden agendas and propaganda. I am a fan of his work and I have an amazing uncle called Jesus. That's my truth and I'm sticking to it.

We are all offshoots of the Prime Creator just like he was. In effect we are all Christ like and I believe he came to show one, out of infinite ways to connect to the God-force buried within each and every one of us. Before him not many of us had seen or heard of a **'natural human being'**, unclogged by human learning, negativity and conditioning. A **natural human being** is one who **expresses unconditional love, is peaceful, consciously connected to a higher level of awareness, self-assured, open, multi-dimensional and fully in touch with what makes them human, a magician and a superhero**. Jesus achieved his status because he displayed all the characteristics coupled with a high level of emotional maturity, and an awareness of his loving God-nature. Something most of us are yet to scratch the surface of.

Being Christ-like or having the 'Christ Consciousness' is a process that helps one align with the gestalt psychology of life, as he's the template some have consented to replicate. It is termed the 'Christ Consciousness' for this reason. Most of the religious bodies acknowledge him based on this too. Jesus is the most cited to have achieved a high state of intellectual development and emotional maturity in recent human history. Personifying the mind-set of unconditional love and blending the ego mind with the divine spirit mind. He is the prototype some seek to emulate, although many others throughout history have achieved what Christ did and more, he made the most impact and he resonates with so many of us on so many different levels. This is the basis of Christianity.

I am very proud of my religious upbringing, as this cause and effect proved vital to the nucleus of my personality. I refer to Christianity often throughout the book because it was my primary building block for belief in a purpose-filled life. It exercised and strengthened my faith in a benevolent force. The reason we gravitate to religion in the first place is because, it contains some of the morals innate in a **natural human being**. I understand that some religious institutions like to think they invented morality, when in actual fact they didn't. Religious books like the Bible, Torah, Gita and Quran however, contain moral gems that will enhance and improve your life if you so desire. Nevertheless, in my opinion they raise more questions and one must be open to seeking some of the answers outside the cultural norms. Religion is an impetus to discover what comes naturally to us. Had I been raised an atheist, believing in a magical charmed Universe might prove a little more challenging. My human experience would have probably been reduced to nothing more than electrical impulses and a concoction of chemicals, believing I was a cosmic joke.

I inherited my positive outlook and enterprising nature from my mother and my keen interest in spirituality from my father. Without trying to sound like a saga longer than The Godfather, Harry Potter and Lord of the Rings combined, I've come to understand and appreciate that, no matter how far back I look there is a cause and effect leading back to the beginning of time, as we know it and beyond, called **infinite regress** that continually shapes the way our lives unfold. Through infinite regress we can see that my job coupled with my spiritual journey were nothing but perfect, to align me with a purpose, hiccups and all. You cannot deny the veracity of purpose driven life. The line of regression steered me right onto your reading list and into your heart. They also revealed so much to me that I thought I wasn't. I certainly didn't think I was insecure, powerless, worthless, angry, fearful and anxious about the world around me.

LIMBO

I am in limbo.
My imaginary place for lost and neglected things.
I am sad, but no one grasps what I am trying to convey.
I resort to melodramatic idiosyncrasies and still nothing.
My plight seems heavy and I need rest.
I am in a state of oblivion!!!
I am bound by expectations.
I am restricted by apprehension. What happens from here?

I am in limbo.
My imaginary place for lost and neglected things.
A fortunate stroke of serendipity might be just what I need to inspire consciousness.

I AM IN LIMBO!!!

Le Feebs

CHAPTER TWO

IF AT FIRST YOU DON'T SUCCEED REDEFINE SUCCESS

It's so easy to get caught up in comparisons and lose your sense of self, purpose and individuality. There came a point in my life where I needed to redefine and appreciate my life for what it was. This was especially true during my time at university. I felt that although I was in further education I was accelerating nowhere fast. I was having a difficult time processing a lot of the illusions that crept into my reality. Here I was, the lone pebble, studying economics amongst a stream of dentists and medics who reckoned they were on

22

their way to saving lives. I was in 'sunny Dee' because my darling mother through emotional manipulation got me to matriculate. If it were up to me I'd have gone to art school and bummed around in London. One of the things my Higher Self highlighted to me was that I had to trust that what was happening to me was necessary and beneficial to my development. In the words of John Lennon in All You Need Is Love, *'there's nowhere you can be that isn't where you're meant to be'*.

I wrote 'Limbo' in an attempt to wake my sleeping mind. I felt terribly unhappy with my choices and developed a habit of 'what if' and started blaming my parents for not giving me better options in life. As a fairly objective individual I, in due course, talked myself out of the mire and embraced the reality I had created. I like to think everybody has a time in their life when they absolutely loathe the process required to accomplish anything. If I had it my way, I'd simply wake up in my desired reality with no effort on my part.

My life completely changed when I finally made the connection that the process and state of limbo were in fact more stepping stones in helping me become the best person I could possibly be and if I enjoyed it, the faster I moved through time (or was it time moving through me?). By redefining the process of studying as necessary, exciting and not a means to an end, I dropped all the resistance, felt lighter and began to have more fun.

In order to help redefine my experience, I had to do four things:

1. **Change my perspective on financial economics and the time spent studying.**
2. **Replace disempowering beliefs with empowering and productive ones.**
3. **Change my actions, behaviour and posture.**
4. **Accept that what was happening was the way it needed to happen.**

I had to do all four things because it was time to learn that **you never change the world, you only change your perspective, which will eventually change your experience**. In my case, graduating in a field I was never zealous about was a miracle in itself as I spent most of my time stuffing my face, getting dumped (I fell for their pelvic sorcery (totally stole this from Gamora in Guardians Of The Galaxy)), stalking my exes on Facebook or sending them long rants about how atrocious they were in emails and texts, 'YouTubing', hanging out, listening to Sandi Toksvig on the News Quiz, and Nicholas Parsons on Just A Minute on Radio 4, watching The Food Network, Come Dine With Me (Dave Lamb is THAT GUY), Shameless, Grand Designs, QI and alas binge on The Big Bang Theory. I think you get the picture now. The list for 'dossing' around in my twenties actually goes on. It was all a very hazy; mind numbing and an uninspired limbo-like experience to plod through and Sheldon Cooper eased my way through most of it. It's fair to say that most of my learning took place on multimedia platforms. Professional slacker comes to mind every time I reminisce about the good old days.

In hindsight some of the actions, which I perceived as detrimental, were quite instrumental in guiding me to the present moment. For instance, The Big Bang Theory, through humour taught me a lot about physics I wouldn't have otherwise been open to and the News Quiz kept me abreast with current affairs in a satirical way. Although I thought I was stuck in an indeterminate state, on closer inspection I was actually getting a well-rounded higher and soul education. I started to be more present, energised and paid more attention in seminars. I began to engage more consciously in class and have a sense of what my degree was about. Eventually I transformed a degree that was on track for a 2.2 to a 2.1 because I chose to open up more and decide that maybe financial economics was not as bad as I previously thought it was.

After graduating, I did the milk rounds and ended up in an investment bank, driven purely by money (like most of my peers) without a thought on how it would impact me holistically. Unknowingly, this environment was perfect for the next phase of my development. I was lucky as far as my employers were concerned as it was a great place and environment to work and develop the mental tenacity necessary to deal with all the various permutations of the stresses of life. There's nothing like a trading desk losing hundreds of thousands a day and directing their anger towards you because somewhere along the lines someone else was negligent.

I graduated three years after the financial crisis in 2010. The global economy in the wake of the '07 mismanagement was becoming more of a joke than an actual form of science and a key to endless prosperity. For the first time in a long time, hegemonies and so-called superpowers were just as clueless about macro managing their economies as the rest of the world. China was calling the shots and owned a ridiculously unsettling number of US Treasury bills. The EU, great in theory, terrible in practice was having major rifts in its monetary union. At the height of the financial boom in London I remember Gordon Brown's very conceited remark in his budget speech saying, 'we will never return to boom and bust'. This was the spirit of the times we lived in and one of the best things to happen was the global recession. It was also very revealing in terms of the 'miss-takes' of our collective understanding of wealth, and its fear based agenda (greed). Our gold reserves had also been sold at an all-time historic low.

Mr. Brown clearly had no idea about the **Law of Relativity, Law of Polarity**, and **Law of Relativity**. There will always be booms and busts because we live in a cyclical and seasonal dimension. Don't want to bore you with the sordid details of the crises as they were well documented by extensive media coverage and numerous enquiries, but I realised that not only was my definition of success redundant, overall it was clear as day to me that the majority of us were making this up as we went along. **That is the beauty about negative, unwanted things in life; they are very clarifying and great for assessment on your way to a happier and better life**.

Growing up I bought into a belief system that said unless you were degree educated in fields such as medicine, law, engineering or accountancy a good secure life was not guaranteed. Society always needed doctors, lawyers, engineers and accountants, but did it really need a confused economist who would have rather preferred to study art? My parents were against me choosing art because they held the notion that I'd become a struggling artist and in a worst-case scenario they didn't want to support me at thirty. I assumed the 'rents' wanted me to develop other steady income producing avenues and so I settled for a degree in financial economics because I figured that if I at least understood how money worked I could still become an artist one day after I had accumulated lots of money and retire on that vineyard somewhere in Burgundy. I also planned to be a shoe designer at some stage in all of this too.

What money and wealth accumulation meant for me was contradictory in my definition at that time. I allowed myself to believe that wealth meant fast cars, big houses, a jet-set lifestyle and arrogant ostentatious displays of money. More and more I understood that **wealth was your ability to do what you needed to do when you needed to do it**. For a long time, I repeatedly heard negative associations with money, which was hilarious because I grew up in a very comfortable extended family unit. Majority of my conditioning was in favour of having a deep pocket over intellectual prowess. My extended family and social circles were very much split over the affair themselves. Those with money ridiculed those with Masters and PhDs, whilst the smart cookies often repeated statements disguised as fact like 'money can't bring you happiness'. One end was the intellectual and the other materialism. Where was the middle ground? I wanted to be successful in life but how was success being defined for me, what did it entail and what levels of success had flourished so far in my family?

Luckily I didn't have to look too far back in history. My maternal grandfather was a Muslim; a northerner in Ghana who was appointed Interior Minister for his constituency in Nkrumah's time. I know very little of my mother's father as I grew up with my father's side. My paternal grandfather was a tycoon in

Ghana and had very little schooling but achieved unparalleled success in his lifetime. I'm talking five wives, Swiss accounts, island hopping, imported Italian marble, staff in uniform, real estate, drivers and various successful business ventures. He was a man that loved to create something out of nothing.

The challenge with his success was that he bore over twenty children and failed to pass on his knowledge or attach a vision of self-sufficiency, love, divinity and unity to his legacy. From that experience with my extended family, I learned that the spirit of self-sufficiency, love, divinity, unity and a trust fund was the most important legacy to leave behind. I am proud of what both my grandparents achieved and I know and understand that they did the best they could with what they had. I am a product of their existence and that is the best legacy anyone can ever leave behind. Both my paternal and maternal grandfathers achieved what my limited mind then defined as success in their lifetime.

I also learned the value of a sound education, but found it was not more valuable than your ability to process and define your life experience. Tutelage alone guarantees nothing but coupled with life experience; both go hand in hand and enhance each other. Looking back, I wish my grandfather wrote a biography, because I believe he understood and lived by some of the principles found in this book and there's so much more I could have learned from him. Nevertheless, life afforded me access to a wealth of information, great experiences, relationships, friendships and opportunities I would have never experienced had I not eventually warmed to my choices and used them as a window to get in touch with certain aspects of my personality. At the very least studying economics enabled me to contribute intelligently at social gatherings and have a firm grasp on the impact of macroeconomic activity on daily life.

Whilst many of my colleagues dabbled in drugs and alcohol, metaphysics found its way to me during my penultimate year at university. Prior to that at sixteen, my cousin introduced me to 'The Secret' on DVD. Intellectually, I made some sense of what they were conveying, although personally I felt the message was shallow and incomplete. It did not resonate with me fully because it failed to address the core empowering beliefs needed to attract this positive, easy, simple life they advertised and we all craved.

For example, repeating a mantra on how attractive and worthy you are without actually believing it from the tips of your hair to the soles of your feet will result in more contempt and doubt, bringing more harm than good. It's very difficult to see the bright side and beauty of anything when you have been chronically accustomed to verbal abuse, violence and negative poverty-ridden illusions.

The 'Law of Attraction' as a standalone law for everything was too far-fetched for me and I felt there had to be more to this. At one level, I appreciated its positive message and on a mass scale it was successful in getting the likes of me to ponder about the general workings of the universal mind. I craved more depth and knew that in time I had to dig deeper in order to experience the life I wanted to create for myself. That time came seven years later when I finally mastered the courage to make the time for some fun internal and external discoveries.

To shed some light on my blasé drug comment, I'm not an advocate for or against alcohol and drugs. These substances both legal and illegal can kill. Why you choose these experiences is what matters. Basically, have a higher purpose for drug and alcohol use other than anxiety, fear and depression because they are extremely disruptive when used incorrectly. I have the occasional tipple as and when and I make sure it's always from a place of joy and happiness. I find that heavy substance users are usually those too scared to face the reality of the life they have subconsciously created or opted for.

My generation is always seeking a new, cheap, fast-hitting substance. To be fair I won't limit this to just my generation. The 90s 80s 70s 60s and beyond were equally dismal with this stuff too. The wackier the concoction, the more they descend on it like a swarm of flies. From acid to glue to bath salts to cough syrup. You name it someone knows how to turn it into a high. They want no responsibility and part in society and on some level this is understandable, you only have to watch the news to see the kind of inconsistent world we have created. Perhaps the greatest risk to humanity's security comes from disaffected young people who then become irresponsible adults. The rising mental health challenges in the UK are a big wake up call for us to focus on developing our intra-personal and existential intelligence.

In tribal clusters and regions, it's noted that some shamans and spiritualists use substances to access certain states of being as gateways into a universal database of unconscious information (the Akash), especially naturally occurring hallucinogens and fermentations. They use it to communicate with spirits. Shamans are usually taught and trained their whole lives before assuming the role of spiritual head in a village or tribe. The knowledge at their fingertips whether you choose to believe in their practices or not makes them qualified to tap into certain conscious gateways that you may not have access to. I'd steer clear of drugs period.

You can't swindle your way into existential knowledge and bliss by lighting a blunt, smoking a pipe or getting pissed.

You have to at least do the mental work sober first. Granted, some natural substances are purely for enhancing energetic cerebral encounters and opening specific conscious gateways, but you literally can't cheat God. Those who are not ready for such encounters may suffer severe mental health consequences from heavy drug and alcohol use either immediately or later on in their lives.

No one does anything unpleasant unless they think it affects them positively in some manner. People turn to drugs because in their belief structure they define that high as more pleasant than daily life, which is usually the deciding factor in fuelling an addiction. Joy and excitement are part of the organising tool kit and principles of life and if you've found it in a bottle, blunt or a pipe instead of yourself, then it stands to reason that a drug will captivate you. The challenges begin when you come down from that euphoria and you have no robust positive views about life and the conscious appreciation for the kindness and generosity all around, you will always need another high to keep you going.

In my opinion, if you're going to rebel (I don't condone it), commit to it wholeheartedly and consciously. That is, if you're going to rob a bank, do it for an insane amount of 100 billion, then I know you mean business. Likewise, if you're going to do drugs, have some boundaries in place. There are drugs of low vibration and high vibration since we're on the subject. In our dimension the **Law of Relativity** makes this possible. If you insist on a high, stick to some home grown substances if I were you and stay away from anything manipulated from its natural state. Just like food loses most of its nutrients during the cooking process most substances undergoing several alterations lose their original intent and vibration. Some drugs will make you feel elated and will have no lasting effects whilst others will increase your level of anxiety over time and make you paranoid. It's your life and your choice. Do prepare yourself for the social, financial, and mental costs of drug and alcohol abuse if this is something you want to explore. Many before you have lost all ties with their family and loved ones because of an addiction.

You will not perceive what you're not the vibration of. That is to say, if you are truly appreciating life as it is, the temptation to escape from reality in the form of drug use, alcohol or any type of addiction will not appeal to you. For me, the joy of self-discovery is one of the best chemical, physiological and empowering experiences I've ever known. I get high, simply by reading a good book, hanging out with the girls, sleeping, a good night out, trying out a new hair conditioner, painting and all that good stuff.

Addiction is a symptom of an unfulfilled life. Don't fall for the allure of the rock and roll lifestyle. It's built on an illusion of lies and many of them suffer from depression. Parents and society can decrease the odds of their kids feeling like this by appreciating life and living their bliss with no fear or prejudice as children can see through lies. Addiction is a mass reflection of society as a whole not dealing with an undesired reality of prejudice, violence, conflict and chronic feelings of unworthiness.

There hasn't been much ground breaking stuff in favour of Class-A drug use but there are always exceptions to the rule. We always know that one person who gets away with everything, even murder (not literally of course). Just look around you for the negative influences rampant in society. The usual culprit; weed, I'm convinced people don't need them half as much as they think and claim they do. There is no judgment here, for all I know you are involved in some higher purpose drug research experiment, don't let me rain on your parade.

Nevertheless, if you do use drugs and want to quit or go cold turkey please seek the help of a qualified, registered professional and change your environment, including friends and sometimes family members who may also be involved in that lifestyle. Birds of a feather...

Oh and stealing is a BIG NO-NO even if it is 100 billion.

CHAPTER THREE

WHAT IS METAPHYSICS?

"Only the truth of who you are, if realised will set you free."

Eckhart Tolle

What is metaphysics and why does it matter?
**Metaphysics is the branch of philosophy that deals
with the first principles of things, including abstract
concepts like being, identity, time and space and
makes up much of the key works of Aristotle.** In
essence it deals with the philosophy of nature, existence and
reality. I don't consider myself a metaphysician but I gravitate
a lot to some of the aspects and theories of existence espoused
by them.

The official term metaphysics is derived from the Greek *Ta Meta Ta Physika*, which means "the books after the books on nature." Quite simply, metaphysics could be translated as 'beyond natural things' as *Meta* means 'beyond' whilst the word *'Physika'* stands for natural things. Metaphysics has become the label for the study of things that transcend the natural world and is most likely the great grandfather 100 times removed from our modern day physics. Much of philosophy is an exercise in some form of metaphysics. We all have a metaphysical perspective because we all form opinions about the nature of reality. Metaphysics is thus important because without an explanation or an interpretation of the world around us we would be helpless to deal with physical reality and normal day-to-day life.

Later on, I expose you to some metaphysical ideas and natural laws to give you an idea of what it's all about. You may not resonate with everything expressed here, nevertheless by learning and applying the natural laws and truths, you can extract from it the things you need, to live a glorious and joyous life. Albert Einstein said *'you have to learn the rules of the game, and then you have to play better than anyone else'*. I say, you **learn the rules of the game of life and play better for yourself**.

If we go back to the definition at the beginning of the chapter, metaphysics talks about dealing with the first principles of things, including how best to exist. 'Being' is an extremely broad concept that has proved elusive and contentious in the history of philosophy but key to understanding the purpose of humanity. How and why the first human being came into existence (the old chicken and egg hullabaloo) still plagues us because our scientific structure is set up to be very sceptical of any religious or Godlike connotations, justifiably due to onus probandi. How do you go about quantifying and proving the existence of something that many are sceptical about? What about humanity, the animals, the planet, how did they all come about and what is their higher purpose? If God exists, are our instruments able to detect and measure the particles that encompass him?

The limitation of being human leaves me no choice but to believe in a higher power, because there is a higher logic and a higher way of thinking that confounds me. I'm also inclined to believe that nothing happens by chance and I find the Universe too logical a place to make living things by accident or randomly. Not even atheists can come up with a logical answer to explain the purpose of humanity. There's too much of an intelligent design to reduce the argument to chaos and chance.

In some branches of metaphysics there's a notion of an intelligent higher force at work throughout the Universe. It doesn't give it an image because our minds will most likely misinterpret, distort and attach a personality-mind to it (*cough religion*). For some, this higher intelligence needs no proof because it is an experience. Humans, nature and consciousness are a product of this intelligence. For others it requires proof because they must see it before they believe in this higher force. For me the Goddess force is everywhere, and She is everyone. She's in everything, every particle, form of matter, atom, electron and proton. The closest we've gotten so far to proving the existence of an intelligent force currently is most likely The Higgs Field, which is subject to change.

The Higgs Field is an energy field that exists everywhere in the Universe much like Creation. The field gives mass to particles by interacting with it and is accompanied by a fundamental particle called the Higgs Boson. The Higgs Boson particle is said to make up the basic building block of things, much like an electron. Many have termed it the 'God particle', due to its elementary characteristics. This particle was initially theorised for 50 years and on July 4 2012; CERN announced its discovery in Switzerland. HOW BLOODY EXCITING! Because our Universe is infinite in nature, I suspect there's probably another elementary particle that makes up the Higgs Boson and going by the rules of cause and effect, we could easily regress it ad infinitum. For more information on the Higgs Boson, Google is your best friend, but I'll leave a link at the end of the chapter for your convenience, thank me later.

The Universe contains a certain level of information that our human understanding cannot fully grasp yet as our collective view of the Universe is most likely rudimentary at best, but our physicists are doing a great job at piecing together some of what they do know.

In my eccentric mind, science and metaphysics go hand-in-hand. Metaphysics identifies Creation as the Source-Energy of All That Is and where everything came from, and science then has the responsibility of unscrambling the hows for those who need proof. This is an introductory text and not an in-depth look at metaphysics, as I won't take the fun of discovery from you. There are many divisions of it but the overall themes of life are unified. As extensions of Source-Energy itself we are therefore creators and have full creative control and responsibility of our personal lives and environment.

The rest of the chapter delves into the metaphysical principles of Creation and theories of how we come into being. As mentioned earlier, when I first discovered 'The Secret' I felt an urge to dig deeper and understand the real message behind it. The search took me on an emotional and intellectual tour I hadn't quite budgeted for. The intellectual and emotional gap of going from a life that just happened to you and playing with the cards you were dealt, to learning that actually you chose and created the cards, was a massive one to overcome. Something happens to your brain when you come from a place of 'somebody is doing this to me' to 'I'm doing this to myself'. Responsibility was a totally different vibe compared to what I was used and it was an adjustment. My transformation took a year and as much as I willed it occur faster, the process didn't budge. With my religious upbringing, a lot of my beliefs and actions were challenged and like a duck to water I rose to it and dealt with some of the underlying fears and the irresponsible choices made in my earlier years.

Some of my findings initially seemed avant-garde, but on closer inspection, they predated the time of Christ and many other religious movements all the way back to the Mystery Schools of Egypt, Asia and probably beyond that too. Bear in mind that your belief systems are the very fabric of your reality and if you contradict them you will experience emotional, physical or mental pain. Therefore, if anything I say proves mind-boggling and goes against everything you have been taught, remember to take what works for you, leave what doesn't and come back to whatever was unclear to you at first glance. There is nothing to fear but fear itself.

I believe we choose our own reality from the unconscious mental world and make certain agreements in the nonphysical/spirit/soul world before you become physical. We are, in effect, spiritual beings having an illusionary Earthly experience. We are created fully as self-sufficient beings, made in the vibration and frequency of unconditional love. All information and human potential is contained in our DNA and there's nothing more intelligent than that. Any time you take your power and remove it from the SELF you deny your very existence and what you have been created to be.

Physical reality is in fact a fantasy and is designed to be perfectly imperfect to keep one's soul entertained and striving for more. In the quest for physical perfection, you can often lose the nuances that made you stand out in the first place (I used to think I wanted a boob job, then I realised that when I died and decomposed, only silicone will be left behind so I made peace with my breasts). It is counterproductive to strive for perfection in physical reality, it doesn't exist and you'll end up in a place of disappointment and frustration if you make perfection your life mission. Absolute perfection lies in spirit, and as a spiritual being, you are already perfect in the eyes of All That Is.

Nothing occurs in your life without a conscious approval on some level. Just because you're not aware of it doesn't negate your part in the sequence of events. If we are to strip down the human form and façade, what you're left with is a body of conscious energy, which governs every part of your physical experience and is omnipresent. The 'electromagnetic theory of consciousness' proposes that consciousness can be understood as an electromagnetic phenomenon. In a sense we're all spheres of moving omnipresent electromagnetic energy fields.

Consciousness governs the brain, the heart and the state of the human form. In fact, consciousness triggers the electrical pacemakers, which causes your first heartbeat. Your conscious state also determines the data received by your biological transmitter (the brain) and receiver (the heart). As ethereal beings, our main ally or foe here in physical reality to our (sub)conscious state is emotion. **Emotion** when broken down further can be interpreted as **energy in motion**. Any action you take then is simply your **conscious energy in motion**.

Because we often perplex ourselves with complex words and language and are predominantly emotionally illiterate, All That Is uses **our actions as an indicator of our true intentions** and how we're really feeling. As creators **what we 'DO' goes.** No ifs buts and maybes, action equals emotion. You cannot say to life that you're passionate about animals, yet you're studying to be a social worker. Actions and not words are how to discern the emotional zeitgeist of your environment. No matter how much you wax lyrical about desiring to be a vet and being bogged down with bills, your ex, or your abandonment issues, your actions are the only indicator of how you truly feel and what's going on with you. Choosing to be a social worker instead of a vet means, you are either too scared to go for what you really want in life or you don't know what you want.

With better emotional literacy, you are more empowered and better able to sort through the illusions of physical reality. Your energy in motion is a major determining factor on the consequences and effects of your mind, body and soul. The emotions (actions) that are most beneficial to your physical form and life are contentment, hopefulness, optimism, positive expectation, enthusiasm, passion and joy as you'll come to find later on, but you are more than welcome to dwell in other emotional states. That is the beauty of free will.

These emotions of contentment and so on generally attract positive circumstances and events for you to sort through. A genuinely happy individual oscillates between all the ranges of emotion from contentment to joy. This doesn't mean they don't get angry, disappointed or frustrated, it means they possess the conscious tools to transform those emotional states to a much a happier state quickly and effortlessly. Through these emotional states, you give consent to many of the circumstances that happen to you. The natural laws will shed some more light on this later on in the chapter. But in summary, **nothing can exist outside of your aggregate conscious thoughts**.

By that reasoning alone, contrary to popular belief we choose everything around us and I mean absolutely everything. You choose your parents, family, friends, era, time frame and physical form by conscious agreements all for a particular purpose (growth and development) in the galaxy. **We also take turns incarnating as men, women, different races, ambiguous life forms in various times and eras to balance out the soul's overall experience.** For the purpose of simplicity, we'll assume these incarnations take place in a linear time frame and not all at once. If all of this sounds too good to be true, at least believe that out of a possible twenty million variations of spermatozoon, one tiny sperm won the right to fertilise the egg that makes up your human form and personality mind. You won, simply by coming into being. So the human story is one of success and not a random chaotic act of the Universe.

Your entry point into Earth doesn't have to be your destination point. As a human being, a global citizen and a galactic resident you have every right to explore and gravitate to whatever way of life you prefer as long as you're not harming anyone in the process (there's the caveat). Countries, regions and unions are clusters of energetic ideas and concepts that may or may not appeal to you or your life theme. If you don't like certain parts of the globe stay away, exercise your free will to remain or leave a cluster you don't appreciate. When you do choose a cluster that appeals to you, accept all the polarities it has to offer and exercise tolerance because ultimately you chose it. If you wish to change something that is dissatisfying to you in that community, use your harnessed 'e-motion' to build something constructive in that society that replaces the outdated belief system you are discontent with. It's much easier to destroy than to build; this is why many resort to destruction and violence as the first port of call because let's face it, they are lazy and want the easy way out. It's always a sign of fear and powerlessness to resort to violence and destruction in an attempt to affect change.

Aggression is a reflection of how helpless you feel. You resort to scaremongering to get attention because you are fearful and incapable of getting what you want. This only attracts more negative illusions, which solves nothing. If you're truthfully after change and not the usual 15 minutes, real transformation requires time, a positive outlook, and a collective constructive effort. **Inspiring change starts with inspiring yourself and reflecting the change you wish to see.** The amount of time it takes to change is relative, depending on the variables and the resistance involved.

If nothing happens without our consent, then it also stands to reason that the time we exit this dimension is also pre-set, give or take a few Earth years or months. If you are born, you have a very high probability of kicking the bucket at some point in time, unless of course you can will yourself away (cue Elijah in the Bible). A cough or a puddle might knock you flat out when heaven calls. You can't cheat death; you might have a grace period for a particular purpose, but when it's your time to go, better believe your higher purpose wins and it's time to go.

On Earth, our physical bodies deteriorate because this process prepares us for death, though the rate at which we age can be slowed down. Our so-called 'modern medicine' can only go so far, because we cannot cure death. Modern medicine can predict someone's ageing process and possible death, provided it has all the necessary information such as lifestyle, job and eating habits. Why can't your higher mind communicate with you when it's time to go (most of us are not ready for this information or prefer not to dwell on it)? Our DNA contains much more information that we are yet to unravel. When it's time to kick the bucket our Higher Self in concert with our body consciousness and the Universe will attract all the circumstances and events to make this happen in a seamless, phenomenal way depending on our dominant thought pattern. We always have the option of changing our minds as there are numerous accounts of near-death experiences, where people were given the option of coming back and living more fulfilling lives. If we want to live longer, healthier lives we must find more peaceful, simple, positive, stress-free ways to consciously live. Ridding our collective mind of extreme violent acts alone will halve the death rate. It's as simple as that.

Knowingly or unknowingly some need the justification of terrible diseases or illness in order for them to transcend into the afterlife. What biologists and chemists don't take into account is that, our souls have lived many incarnations and each life passes on its cell memory and information. Our body/DNA contains the potential for every disease known to man, past, present and future. Even if we eradicate all forms of ailments, because of our set up here on Earth, when it's your time to die your body consciousness can spark something out of remission to move you on to your next adventure. No one actually dies; we merely change from one form to the next.

Others attract very violent or seemingly random circumstances and events, whilst some peacefully die in their sleep in the guise of old age. Death by old age is the most widely accepted and most celebrated form of leaving the game of life socially. Personally, I relish the thought of ageing. Growing old has an added advantage as it brings its own quirks. In your old age, you shed the mental inhibitions of youth and are finally free to be yourself. I quite fancy myself a fun-loving, grumpy old woman, if that's in my soul's plan as rudeness is somewhat amusing in old age.

Some may also choose to take their own lives when life understandably gets dull, tough, or no other apparent option presents itself. Suicide is never the answer, yet the choice is always yours and we must respect such decisions. We live in a world where depression exists and some people don't have the required emotional tools to deal with the unwanted illusions they have created. We are taught to be happy in happy times, but are we taught the same in trying times? Life on Earth is not for every soul; one's temperament might just be better suited to other eras, centuries, planets or dimensions.

Death is a taboo topic in society and yet it's something we will all face eventually. We always act extremely shocked and brand new when someone passes on, like it's the worst affliction ever. I empathise with the loss of a loved one, especially when it could have been prevented, but to take it personally, wear a badge of grief and worry has never been one of my greatest strengths because I believe death is not the end and no one dies without their unconscious permission anyway. For those who think otherwise, I can appreciate the impact of the loss (sudden or gradual). I like to think your loved ones are willing you to move on from the grief and live the life you deserve. Truth is we were always on borrowed time. It's imperative to make the life in your years count and in doing so the notion of a premature death disappears.

We are also more in control of our outcome and environment more than we have been conditioned to think. **Ideally there shouldn't be a masculine, feminine or race agenda just a human one and yet here we are**. To idolise and promote one gender, race or religion in favour of another to is to discredit the validity of everything life has to offer. Some or all of you might be reading this and thinking why would anyone want to be born into poverty, abuse, a conflict zone or an undesirable circumstance? I say why not? All those descriptions and labels provide variety and an added advantage to the human experience if you choose to see it that way. If you came to Earth via those conditions surely you came with the mind to transform that energy into something productive and shine your light of awareness for the good of all humanity. We all take turns in being teachers and students in each other's lives for our soul's development. Due to the state of our collective conscious mind on Earth, someone has to reflect these terrible things in order for us to shake up our laws and our thought processes. Your experience alone might inspire or spark new waves of thought and inventions that will advance civilisation. You can make sure whatever complaints you have, they never happen again by either passing laws, finding solutions, writing books, composing soothing music, teaching the alternative, starting foundations, educating and empowering the masses; the possibilities are literally infinite. We're constantly made to feel guilty about every poor decision we make in society, when in fact some of these terrible decisions have paved the way for some of the great things we have in the 21st century and beyond.

I'm all for giving back, but poverty is not the opportunity to hold those with money responsible, or to be held at ransom for your life. This isn't to say all rich folk made their money through moral means. I'm not referring to them here and we live in a world where moral distress is not the same as legal distress and negligence costs (I've learned that the hard way many times). This is why it's very important to be very self-aware and conscious of the part you play in any and every situation. Be aware of your motives at all times. Being born poor doesn't mean you have to stay poor unless you choose to wear it as a badge of honour or use it for your own creative purposes. The reality is if we took all the money in the world and shared it equally amongst all 7 billion of us, some will still end up being richer than others because of their thought processes. Whilst some are busy spending it, others will be busy creating products and avenues of expenditure, so our collective understanding of poverty needs a shake up from the neck up (pardon the cliché). It's not a divide between the 'haves' and the 'have nots' but rather those who feel worthy and thus empowered and abundant versus those who don't. If you believe you are worthy and deserving of all good things, you're more likely to take care of yourself and your environment. You will reach out for all the great things life has to offer and more.

On the other hand, if you chose to be born with a title and silver spoon in your mouth and you're done playing 'Richie Rich', you can help kick start and bankroll a lot of these life-changing foundations that the other half inspire or simply doss about. There are no hard and fast rules on how to spend your money, but be mindful of the causes and effects in every action or inaction. Doing nothing with your wealth will most likely lead to poverty, if that's the illusion you're after. The Universe gladly allows all choices.

If it's only money you're after, getting it is far simpler than we have been conditioned to think. Wealth is an outcome of a chronic, appreciative, abundant thought pattern. I like to think we all know by now that, hard work alone does not translate to prosperity. I know a lot of people who work extremely hard for their income and although they're happy and comfortable, it's not synonymous with a deep pocket. The definition of **wealth** and abundance I adhere to is **your ability to do what you need to do when you need to do it.**

Money is the result of placing value on one's energetic output. The more value you provide the more energy you'll receive in return. The Universe doesn't favour one form of energy over another. When sending a message out to the Universe there is no such thing as too big. It takes the same amount of energy to manifest a pebble as it takes to manifest billions. If you don't want to exchange money for something of value, it's always free if you do it yourself. It's not Decepticon science. Once someone else uses their energy to create something of value for you, you have to compensate them for that energy exchange and the accepted legal medium of exchange in the 21st century is MONEY. Gone are the days of the barter system of salt, and agriculture. Try paying your landlord or your employees with a fruit basket and see how far that gets you. I know on a micro, tribal and personal level there is a barter or favour system, but they use the same principles as money, i.e. create something of value and be compensated accordingly by some form of mutual agreement.

Jonathan Randolph Price called money: **M**y **O**wn **N**atural **E**nergy **Y**ield. You create money or value from the energy you expel. Consequently, money can be reduced to energy. Money is a medium of exchange, a measure, a standard and a store. It's also an illusionary, transient effect of a cause; if you want vast sums of it, create a cause with your natural energy and support it 100%. **The effect of accumulating lots of money is the outer symbol of whatever you have going on consciously**. Money is a very neutral energy field and when tapped into, gravitates to those who have a balanced or positive view about it and know what to do with it when it shows up. It compounds pretty quickly too. You go where you're celebrated so why can't money? Granted some can be very 'look at me' with their vast sums of money, but it's their choice. People are entitled to do whatever they want to do with their money. If you can't deal with that then there might be some deeper issues and underlying beliefs going on that you need to have a closer look at.

Accumulating tonnes of cash is not a hall pass to let your ego run rampant because you think your bank balance defines you. It's time we stopped glorifying anything, let alone financial wealth like it's the second coming of Jesus. Having money doesn't automatically translate to a great sense of self-worth or accomplishing a great feat in humanity. A personality is something you have to develop and has nothing to do with your bank balance. In fact, you can always spot those with money and no personality. They were totally misinformed about money bringing joy, satisfaction and admiration. They assumed having money meant true love when in fact it attracted gold diggers, fraudsters, liars and users. Know who you are outside of acquiring wealth. That way when it comes, you don't become unrecognisable, seeking validation from everything money can buy. The same people who supported you when you had nothing are most likely the same people who will be there when your financial illusion disappears. Appreciate those close to you and around you.

If you're after a page in the history books for your contribution to humanity, which I suspect most people are, you'll need to be driven by enthusiasm, joy and love and not the illusionary effects of money such as fast cars, gadgets, jets, men and women. Most of us are chasing the opposite and putting the cart before the horse. The toys come after you know who you are, unless of course you value illusions and the superficial over substance. *"Nowadays people know the price of everything and the value of nothing."*- Dorian Gray (Oscar Wilde)

There is no rulebook on which causes generate the most money; in fact, it doesn't even have to make sense to make money. Each choice or cause contains the amount of energy equal to the degree of expression. That is to say, if your energy can drive it all the way, it will most likely go all the way, provided you have no limiting beliefs, emotions and people's expectations holding you back. The number of honest income producing jobs and businesses out there are actually staggering. These days, you can find a Gin Tailor, to help you brew bespoke gin (I mean I couldn't make this up if I tried). Think Facebook, and mull over exactly why its founder is worth over 20 billion dollars for a minute. Not to take away from his success, just illustrating a point that we didn't even know we needed or wanted Facebook till Mark Zuckerberg created it. In hindsight, Facebook is ground breaking. There was no market research for that path of financial success for

Zuckerberg, just a trail of failed social networking sites like Hi5, Bebo, and MySpace.

Likewise, take sports in general or more specifically football (Red Devils for life). Eleven men set aside to kick a ball around and perhaps score a goal in some sort of polygon contraption, has grown into a billion-dollar business, which makes no bloody sense, yet it feeds and caters a percentage of humanity. There is no discrimination, if you're passionate enough about it, remain open, with no attachments to the outcome, it will have social impact and make your bank account grow too. Don't take my word for it just watch the Rise of Super Star Pets on Channel 4, or even the meerkats from comparethemarket.com. The Universe always uses your natural talents and leanings (usually the path of least resistance) to provide through you and for you. Your flairs, passion, and excitements are usually laden with zero, or the least amount of, mental resistance or negativity and when developed, yield unfathomable results.

If wealth is not the goal and it really doesn't have to be, you can also choose to twiddle your thumbs and take it easy in this incarnation and not engage in anything. The choice is really yours and the possibilities are endless. What makes you think a seemingly lost, aimless soul is not enjoying that topsy- turvy experience on a deeper level? Granted, a lot of us have not fully developed our self-awareness, but you can't make accurate judgments about people's lives and choices and assume you know what's best for them, until you speak to them. A shared understanding of a problem brings about a unified solution for it. For all you know, some of these 'lost souls' are on a break in between lifetimes. This is probably recommended to recharge the soul. Not everybody wants the G650s, a palace, a Hennessey Venom GT, a JustGiving page, a stylist on call and a Google alert page (personally I can handle the first two).

When you have many lifetimes and eternity to complete anything, one Earth lifetime in the grand scheme of things is a joke at best. Makes you wonder why we all rush through life? Rush to fall in love, to get into jobs we detest and compete to keep up with the Joneses we can't stand (my apologies to anyone called Jones as there's no need to disparage others to make a point). We forget about what really matters and isolate those around us because we fear our own divinity. The reality is, everything is always in the state of evolution. The catalogue is endless for the numerous reasons why you choose certain conditions, but I think the most exciting thing is finding out that you chose it and that your soul has 100% creative control.

Have you ever met someone who seemingly had it all materially and suddenly lost it all? On a deeper level they were after a challenge, something to transmute and keep them preoccupied. A life without tests is a life without growth. Why should those with money miss out on the fun of growth and learning? You come here to exercise your creative metaphysical muscles and for a short time (Earth years) conveniently forget your true identity. In other words, after spending some time on the third rock from the sun you undoubtedly graduate with a PhD in creativity or whatever high honours you can achieve on Earth so we all win no matter what. If you get it wrong, you always have the option of coming back to correct whatever you think went sour because it's all an illusion.

Not to make light of these issues, I just want you to understand that poverty, abuse, conflict, and money are just illusions and not a life sentence. Growing up, my nuclear family went from one extreme to the other. Coming from a state of mind where everything was done for you by a chef, driver and maid, to living on £10 a month and sharing a two-bedroom flat because that was all we could afford at that time. Before then, I had no concept of lack, but it was clearly floating around somewhere in the mind of my parents. We went from an abundance of abundance to an abundance of lack and that greatly impacted me. My sense of self was caught up in someone else's achievement and my infamous family name. This was probably one of the most creative times in my life as **there's nothing like a money shortage to stimulate creativity and promote self-determination and self-sufficiency**. I've had some innovative moments with no food in my belly.

At present, due to a series of conscious choices, I'm sharing a house with three strangers, a gazillion spiders and one black mouse (who is partial to Snicker bars, he/she won't go near a Rich Tea biscuit). The communal bathroom and kitchen leave a lot to be desired, but I've accepted this is where I am and therefore where I need to be. With no income stream, my mum and I opted to downsize whilst I 'found myself'. The alleyway from the high road to my doorstep is another story entirely. I can make a song and dance about how dreadful this is, but I find the whole thing side splitting. I attracted this temporary illusion purely for stimulation and it has definitely served me well. I know that if I left London, I could rent a house for the same price we're paying for two single rooms in a shared house, but London is home and there's nowhere I'd rather be. The truth is, with humans when we're pushed; we're stronger and creative. How else would this tale and experience have come about?

Remember that reflections of lack are simply your consciousness alerting you about your belief in a limited flow of energy or to spark ingenuity, you decide how best it serves you.

For more information on metaphysics, Google or other ancient mystery books are your friends. One I used was www.importanceofphilosophy.com.

For more information on the Higgs Boson visit: http://www.sparknotes.com/mindhut/2013/10/08/faq-higgs-boson-for-dummies.

CHAPTER THREE (A)

THE PRINCIPLES OF
METAPHYSICS

*"Man suffers because he takes seriously what the gods made
for fun."*

Alan Watts

The Universe is a very orderly place, where nothing occurs by chance. Most of the metaphysical principles you are about to encounter seem obvious, because they are. They work whether you believe in them or not. You may not believe in the laws of gravity but you certainly feel its effects every time you jump up. They apply to everything and everyone and can be used to enhance the practice of any faith or ideology.

I'd like to think it does what it says on the tin and it's no respecter of persons. You can be green, blue, black, yellow, short, tall, brown, confused, straight, transgendered, gay, skinny or fat, round; square or thin (catch my drift?). Every generation has their conscious agenda, mandate, style, execution and form. Sometimes they remix something from the past but the fundamental principles remain the same.

For best results: focus on one principle at a time. Don't overwhelm yourself by trying to perfectly apply every piece of information at once. As you learn about each principle, study those around you. Watch television, and news segments with a more critical eye, and pay close attention to how they play out in your everyday life. See if you can pinpoint where and when others have used these principles to create events and circumstances in their lives both positive and negative. Study yourself and become aware of your own conscious and unconscious ulterior motives. After a while I am certain you'll come to appreciate that we live in a world where everything is just, connected and works effectively. As you expand and grow, they will become second nature to you.

Let's get stuck in with my interpretation of these laws in no particular order apart from the first four. The rest is tautology clothed in semantics to further explain the nuances of life.

1. The Law of 'Mentalism'

"The All is mind; the Universe is mental."

Everything we experience in physical illusionary reality is first conceived in the invisible mental realm of consciousness. You are part of a planet conscious Earth mind and on a broader scale a universal mind from which all thought forms express themselves. From the collective mind, all things manifest. Therefore, as a physical being you must have been a non-physical entity in the greater mind of All That Is.

2. Law of Existence

Your soul/spirit exists, you can't change that, you might change form for various reasons, space-time, time-space and dimensions, and hence in some shape of form you will always exist. **The only stipulation is you have never been this 'YOU' before**. Remember, death is an illusionary process to transport you back into the invisible mental realm you came from. Stop arguing with Creation, if you exist you deserve to exist. Creation supports your existence and in whatever shape or form that may be. You are worthy and valuable to Creation and there is no use disputing this fact. It's is never true that you're unworthy and undeserving because you exist. Your existence proves your worth and purpose.

3. The Law of One

Everything in the Universe is far more connected than you will ever appreciate from your current viewpoint. This law states that '**the one is all and all are one**'. In other words, we all collectively make up the image of The Prime Creator. This includes trees, plants, insects, ocean, rivers, amoeba and a whole bunch of other conscious life forms. Everything is from the Goddess. Every part, no matter how tiny or seemingly insignificant is the whole expressing itself as part of the whole. We, in simple terms, make up the sum of the whole. You are interlinked with all thought forms, all consciousness, all civilisations, all eyes, all ideas, all minds, all hearts, all soul, all spirit is one and you are part of it. All things contribute consciously and unconsciously to what happens on our planet with our mental mind. Your invisible mental mind does a lot of the talking on your behalf in human affairs. For humans, most of the unconscious part is assimilated in dreamtime, when your soul communicates uninterrupted with All That Is (and you thought you were just sleeping). We also dream to expel a lot of creative energy and play with possible outcomes (I wanted to go skiing last year, but every dream I had concerning the slopes involved an accident. That was my cue to postpone this desire and let it go for now, there was also that tiny detail of funds).

4. Law of Change

Everything changes bar the first three laws, mentalism, existence, and the law of one. You cannot change the fact that you exist; you are consciousness and part of Creation.

5. Law of Vibration

Absolutely everything in the Universe moves and thus vibrates. Nothing rests. This concept applies to your thoughts feelings and desires and physical surroundings too. Every thought, feeling, desire has its own unique frequency and when tuned, attracts like unto itself. How you feel indicates your vibration in that moment. If you do something in a feeling of anger you are most likely going to attract angry and frustrated illusions. It's important to think about your emotions and your vibrations before you venture out into any action or activity. You, as a being, have your own distinctive electromagnetic frequency, which is emitted out at every heartbeat that scientists are calling L-energy. You send out an exclusive vibratory signal to space, the galaxies, and the milky ways combined. We are all connected through vibration and resonance.

There's more info on L-energy in The Heart's Code by Paul Pearson that illustrates how the heart's energy communicates to us and to the Universe around. There's a lot of nonverbal communication going on that we haven't yet cottoned onto. It's metaphysics with supportive qualitative and quantitative data. I'm still 57% of the way through it on my Kindle app since 2013 but I recommend it if you're more scientifically inclined.

- **Law of Sympathetic Resonance**

When two people meet, whoever has the dominant vibration or electromagnetic field will influence and perhaps determine the outcome of that interaction. The person with the less dominant vibration will match the one with the most dominant vibration. In addition, when two people are of similar vibration patterns and are attracted to each other, they feel this attraction because they are in resonance. You may also use this to improve a particular skill. For example, sportsmen use this idea to train with the best in the world to improve their skill in their field. It's also the underlying motivation for a mentor or a guide. This law is also apparent when tuning string instruments or pianos.

6. Law of Correspondence

Our outer world is a reflection of our inner world, as within, so without, as above so below. Whatever vibrational frequency you give off is what you get back. It is a mirror, a reflection of your accumulated beliefs feelings and thoughts. If you desire change in your outer world, you must first change your beliefs, thoughts and feelings in your inner world. When you change them, the outer world has no choice but to change to your new belief and frequency.

7. Law of Belief

Whatever you believe, with feeling and conviction becomes your reality. It is not until you change your beliefs that you change your reality. Believing is seeing, because you support your beliefs with data and not the other way round. Beliefs don't have to be rational. It's just that, a belief. Beliefs have a reinforcing mechanism that locks itself in place. Your belief has to be converted into action, if you're not acting it out you most likely don't believe or support it. If you've picked up a belief that says the colour of your skin affects your economic output, guess what? It's going to be true for you.

Think of beliefs as the three-legged stool in Figure 1. The flat surface at the top represents the belief that race affects salary. The legs represent the supporting data that reinforces it and gives it legs to stand on. The supporting data can be, 'I didn't get the job because I was black', or 'there aren't many representations of rich black folk so I can only amount to so much'. Finally, the third supporting data will be, 'white people control the world and they don't want black people to amount to anything because there's a race conspiracy going on'.

Ridiculous and stereotypical, I know but this is how a lot of people filter their life experiences and have legs to stand on. Not to dispute the fact that there aren't racists in this world, but they can't affect your state of being and therefore your magnetic nature unless you let them. They have no business in your reality and it's by invite only.

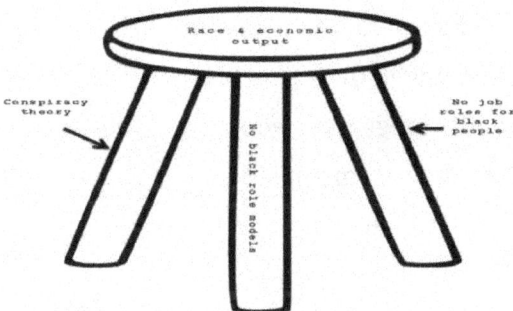

Figure 1

In order to get rid of this belief entirely you must remove the supporting data. In this case there are obviously plenty of black or ethnic role models in society we can learn from so that negates this belief and the stool begins to wobble. Poverty is obviously not colour or gender specific whilst we're on the matter. It affects consciousness not form. Also you can never actually model your whole life on others. Maybe on some aspects but not the whole picture because you are unique so the idea of needing a role model is bonkers. You go through this mental process of elimination until your beliefs have nothing to stand on like in Figure 2.

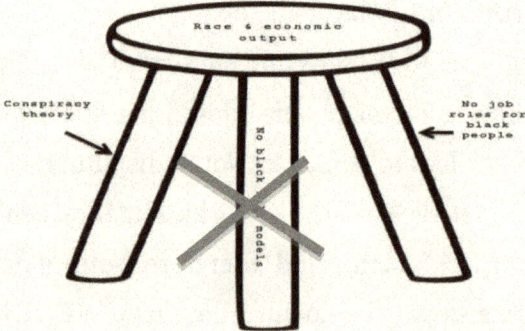

Figure 2

This reinforcing mechanism works with every life decision you make too. When you decide to leave a relationship, the belief that held you in that situation for longer than necessary will start to rear its head with things like, 'you may not be happy, but at least you have someone to cuddle in the winter', 'someone is better than no one', 'you can't have it all' or 'you don't deserve any better'. This is not a sign of weakness but the mechanism doing its job to keep you in that illusion. When you realise that it's just an illusion and you can render it futile, all the doubts and resistance will disappear, because YOU, and not the belief, are in control of your life decisions.

- **Law of Expectation**

  Whatever you expect with absolute confidence is what will manifest in your reality. If you believe and expect that good things will happen, they will. What we expect from people around us, determines how they will inevitably interact with us.

8. Law of Control

Your self-esteem is equal to the degree of control you feel you have in your life.

I. Law of Accident

This is inversely related to the law of control. You will have a low self-esteem to the degree that you feel you are in control of your life. When everything is going your way, you feel happier and more powerful.

When shit hits the fan, the whole world is against you.

9. Law of Attraction

This law is how you create the props, characters and drama in your life. Beliefs, thoughts, feelings and objects have magnetic energy, which attracts like matter unto itself and ultimately the life you want to create. Contrary to popular belief you don't think thoughts. Thoughts come to you based on the vibrational frequency you emit. In essence you tune into certain though patterns based on your current emotional state and your conscious level of awareness. You are basically a living magnet. If it's something that you want, give it more energy and attention and if it's something unwanted give it less attention. This law is not a standalone law and works alongside all the others. If you persistently believe you are unloved and worthless, only miserable thoughts and circumstances will continue to find you, albeit you'll have moments of joy. Your life experience will feel like hell on Earth. Your dominant beliefs, thoughts and issues will always affect the outcome of a situation. You keep yourself from having better things in life by the thoughts that you entertain.

10. Law of Action

Action is motion in your desired direction and outcome. Any action you take is complementary to your beliefs and way of life. It is an expression of your true intention and desire to the environment and Universe. All action is energy in motion. Any time you act out what's in your head you make it seem more real and tangible, as you are focused in a very physical way. Think about what excites you and do it. Act because there's nothing else you'd rather be doing with no insistence on an outcome. Actions make the invisible visible; hence you must engage in actions that support your request. By consistently simulating as close as possible the feelings your imagination conjures up when you think about the life you most want, you radiate an energy that says this is who I really am and you bring it into fruition over time.

Side note: Being busy and filling your life with activity is not what this law is about. They say *'only the person at peace with himself can enjoy the gift of leisure'*. Often times through a misinformed perspective, we incorrectly label being idle, standing still and resting as laziness. They assume that the extremely busy person is the most productive when it's not necessarily the case.

If you look at Newton's first law of motion, action differs for everyone depending on your point of view, because inactivity is also an action. It's imperative to pause and ponder where you are and which direction you are going in life because direction is always more important than speed. That pause can take days, weeks, months or even years. This is a point of power as your reality can move in any direction you want it to once you can clearly outline and define where you're headed. Only you know what your life needs.

Newton's first law of motion says an *object viewed in an inertial reference frame either remains at rest or moves at a constant velocity unless acted upon by an external force.* By way of explanation, if you are in equilibrium with the rate of speed of the object it can appear to be standing still similar to a stroboscopic effect, or moving at a constant speed, it is all relative. You make your assumptions on an object based on your reference point. This bears no truth as to what's actually going on with the object.

The second and third laws are as follows:
II. The force (f) on an object is equal to the mass (m) and acceleration (a) of that object.
$f = ma$
III. For every action there is an equal and opposite reaction.

11. Law of Cause and Effect

Nothing happens by chance or outside of the universal laws. This law states that absolutely everything happens for a reason. The choices you make are causes, conscious or unconscious depending on your inherent beliefs will produce a corresponding effect. Every action has a reactionary result or consequence. St Augustine said it best with this, *"there is no such thing as a miracle which violates natural law; there are only occurrences which violate our limited knowledge of natural law."* Specifically, just because there's no plausible explanation, doesn't negate its cause on a mental level somewhere in the Universe.

12. Law of Compensation

Every day is a day of accumulated compensation. Whatever dominant thought or vibe you put out is what you are compensated with on a daily basis. Our society places a great emphasis on money alone as the obvious effects of a prosperous outlook, when it's just the one of many ways God provides for us. Other visible effects of our collective thoughts and actions are given to us in the form of family, friends, relationships, creative pursuits, peace, contentment, self-expression, confidence, laughter, gifts and toys.

Much like the law of cause and effect, and correspondence, this law permeates most of human activity whether we are aware of it or not. This also applies to blessings and abundance in cause and effects.

13. Law of Perpetual Transmutation

Everyone has within them the power to change all conditions in their life. Higher vibrations of love consume and transform lower ones of hate and fear. This simply means that there will always be an area in your life that needs work. This will come in the shape of your relationship with yourself, work, health, friends, family, partner, children and colleagues. You will always have the opportunity to shine your light of love on it and transform it into something desirable for you.

14. Law of Relativity

Each conscious being on their Earth journey will have a series of challenges/tests/initiations for the purpose of strengthening the light within. Remaining connected with your heart (our biological antennae), helps you solve problems that arise and put things into perspective. It tells us that everything in our physical illusionary reality is made real by its comparison or relationship to another. Heat exists because we compare it to the cold. Health is only valuable when you're ill. People tend to change when their situations get relatively worse. All things in life have no inbuilt meaning until you compare it to another. Nothing is really good until you introduce a relative difference to it.

15. Law of Polarity

Everything has an opposite; therefore, everything is dual in nature. Hot and cold, big and small, good and bad, positive and negative, rich and poor, advantage and disadvantage, integrated and segregated. The mere presence of a cold sensation is an indicator that in order to feel a hot sensation you must increase the number of vibrations to heat up the air molecules around you. This is done either via increased movement or a radiator. It's up to you to turn to and focus on the polarity you wish to multiply in your life.

16. Law of Duality

Dual means two, therefore duality means there are two sides to everything, just like polarity, but this is here for further clarification. All aspects of duality are equal. In every situation in life, under duality, you are simply seeking to balance the duality. Hot is not better than cold. Neither is big better than small. Positive and negative are equal based on your preferences. Under duality, good and evil are one and the same, because there really is no source of evil in this universe, only love allowed or disallowed. You can buy low and sell high or sell high and buy low. They are really the same activity. Law of relativity and polarity go hand in hand.

17. Law of Rhythm

Everything vibrates and moves to certain rhythms, established seasons, time-space and space-time continuums, patterns, cycles and stages of development. Each pattern reflects the regularity of the Universe (think the golden ratio, Fibonacci sequence, fractals, 528 Hz music and many more). Those who have mastered these laws and principles know how to rise above the negative and unwanted cycles by not focusing on unwanted polarities and remaining neutral in those cycles. When that wave of momentum is back on their preferred reality they ride that wave and lay some foundations, which will carry them through the next/future downturns.

18. Law of Gender

Everything has a masculine and feminine energy or essence because everything has an opposite. In order for something to exist it must have unity with the male and female aspects of Creation. To create you need both the masculine principle (seed) and feminine principle (womb/incubator) to manifest. The masculine represents the idea (sperm), freedom of expression and the gestation; incubation or nurturing aspect of the idea represents the female. It's in the womb the other half of the idea (baby) is fertilised, grows receives love, care, nourishment and when it's ready to manifest, delivers. The masculine principle is the conscious part of an idea. The feminine principle is the life giving energy.

Mother Nature is referred to as such, because taking time out in nature restores life in you. Her essence is captured in femininity.

Individuals have both masculine and feminine energies in their makeup, as this is vital for creativity. In the process of evolution, we seek out the opposing energies in our make-up, i.e. the masculine seeks the feminine and the feminine seeks the masculine in order to feel more of your true nature. Remember, in every situation in life, under duality, you are simply seeking to balance the duality. The full development of the masculine side helps us take charge of our careers, provide for ourselves and go out and get what we want from life. The full development of the feminine side means you are able to see yourself as part of the whole. You place a value on everything around you. You operate in ways that benefit yourself and the whole. When we develop enough spiritual depth, we realise that what we seek in others, we really seek in ourselves and we begin to balance and depend on ourselves more. Eventually we reach a point where we no longer depend on others or ourselves, and become channels for unconditional love and light to shine through. You relax in your chosen essence and remain open to all possibilities. **You choose then to play any role you want in society because you can and because it's fun. This is the ultimate stage of awareness**. There really are no pre-assigned gender roles or preferred sexual orientation just ones based on culture, and its norms, which vary greatly over time and space. How you live your life and who you have sex means nothing to Creation as long you are happy, do it consciously with consent and harm no one in the process.

19. Law of Paradox

When you stop needing anything or stop insisting on a particular outcome and let go of attachments and relax, everything you have always wanted and have been searching for will find you. For example, have you ever lost something and you actively went searching for it and found nothing? The minute you pour yourself a glass of wine and put your feet up, you get a flashback and suddenly remember where you put it. That's the law of paradox at work. I.e. whatever you're searching for is also searching for you.

20. Respect for all life forms

It's important to value all life forms around us. I added this because this is something we all conveniently forget when it suits us, including myself of course. Our egos may not agree with or like everything we observe or hear people say, but the heart of respect calls us to hold all things dear and valid. Under no circumstance should a fellow being be physically violated. As per the **Oxford Dictionary, a violation consists of breaking or failing to comply with the law or a formal agreement, failing to respect someone's peace or privacy or to treat someone with irreverence disrespect or assault**. Our very limited understanding of the Universe calls us to take a step back and let things be unless of course whatever ever is being witnessed is being done with malicious intent and excessive force to cause bodily harm or mental distress to another.

In spite of respecting all life forms, most of us are omnivores, until we evolve to photosynthesise our food, this is the only time we can cut plants or put animals down for the purpose of energy exchange (food). Yes, vegetarians, plants are also conscious beings, enough with the intolerant agenda and allow all to co-exist (I should know since I used to be one). There are many humane and respectful ways to kill for food on Google if that sort of thing excites you.

This law also easily ties with the wonderful **law of minding your own business**. By all means, even when it hurts to stay away from the deliciously, gory details of someone else's personal life, refrain from digging too deep and commenting (I'm still working on this). A high level of mental awareness comes with a high level of mental courtesy. Unless you are on speed dial with All That Is concerning their higher purpose or they seek your counsel it is best to maintain an objective emotional distance. People have their reasons and agendas for the pain and joy they gravitate to and from. Do not get distracted and start picking sides. When the dust settles the messenger is shot as a result of meddling. Remember this is all an illusion. There's good in evil and evil in good.

The Big Take Away...

When you really understand the workings of these laws you will find comfort in the fact that you no longer harbour ill will, resentment, anger and disappointment because you ultimately take creative responsibility for the way things turn out. Pardon the use of masculine pronouns here but in essence the cheat, cheats himself, the liar, lies to himself, the abuser, abuses himself, and the thief steals from himself, from the gift of unconditional abundance, light, love and truth. You can trust in the fact that the laws that govern life will even and balance it all out. Anytime you exploit, manipulate or steal something from someone, you effectively take away from your natural energy field. Future endeavours with the rest of humanity will end up costing you more financially, socially and mentally because of your underlying fears.

Secondly you are empowered to change whatever it is you say you don't want, because you now know how to get rid of unwanted beliefs. You focus only on loving thoughts because you ultimately want to attract only love into your life, because ultimately (say it with me), 'THOUGHTS BECOME THINGS!'

It might be a light bulb moment for you now as people's true intentions begin to make sense to you. Most of what we do falls into this mental framework. An insecure person believed the lie about their irrelevance to humanity. The thief couldn't trust that his or her own efforts could provide for them and so went about taking from others. The liar erroneously believed that he wasn't enough as a person and had to be someone else in order to be accepted and live a successful life. They were all coming from a place of fear and feelings of inadequacy. **Fear is blind. We hold on to things, beliefs and limitations out of the fear that we don't deserve better. Love is all seeing and all knowing. It evolves and allows all things to be**. You start to see things as they really are and not what you want them to be and no one can hurt you without your permission and full cooperation. You realise that it's not so much that some people are luckier than others, but rather these folks have less hindering, fear-based beliefs holding them back.

All of these principles can be collapsed into roughly four or five laws. Have fun collapsing them and contact me with a breakdown of your summarised laws. If you want more elaborate expansion on these laws have a look at *The Kybalion,* in my opinion it's one of the best places to start if this isn't esoteric enough for you. Don't feel overwhelmed when you dive into it, it has the potential to do that for some reason. The trick is to read it once, leave it alone and go about your business. As excitement prompts you to read it again, do it and all will begin to make sense in a deep cell memory kind of way. I also recommend Googling these laws in your search bar. There are some very informative blogs and websites that expand on these laws too. For no particular reason I like www.one-mind-one-energy.com/12-universal-laws.html last

visited on 26th July 14. Additionally, try
http://www.whatismetaphysics.com/universallaw.html last
visited on 14th September 14.

One more thing, while we make all these choices to procreate, we must do so responsibly and out of love and care to the environment around us. We all have a level of choice and free will, yet when you make that choice to procreate it's not something to take lightly. I'm mostly speaking to women, who make that ultimate choice to nurture life in their wombs and become primary caregivers.

Bringing a child into this world is a huge, selfless undertaking, a lifelong commitment and should not be done on a whim. The urge to create life is magical and is best done when both parents have a firm grasp on who they really are, what they stand for and an understanding of what it involves, because so much of the parent's beliefs, mental framework and cell information are passed on to the child and creates a cycle. Please don't make this decision because you think having a child will validate you as a woman, dressing them up is cute, will make your partner stay, love you more or give you access to his wealth, and if you're in a welfare state, give you housing and benefits (I know some of us like to think it's the State's job to care for our kids and have all sorts of ulterior motives for creating life). More often than not, children can complicate relationships, as your focus is on the child and no longer on your partner.

In my opinion every woman or man should always factor in the possibility of one parent leaving before making their minds up about kids because honestly these are the times we live in and people's words and actions no longer match. The natural guilt for not caring for your child will haunt you for a lifetime. It's just one of those things. Furthermore, factor in the probability that your child may have completely different needs and requirements, than what you expected or are used to. What screws us up the most in life is the picture in our head of how things are supposed to be. Each child comes with its own set of challenges to propel you as a parent and the collective mind into the next growth phase and make us better loving beings. Love is letting those we love be themselves; otherwise we love only the reflection of ourselves that we see in them. We all have a responsibility with the level of care, love and education we pass on to the next generation. It's up to you primarily as a parent to give your child the necessary skills to participate in the game of life, and if you as an adult haven't developed it how can your children thrive in this environment?

There are options available for those who change their minds about an unwanted pregnancy. Heck, there are many things you can do to prevent pregnancy in the first place. This is the twenty first century. Please visit your local health clinic for more information on the various types of protection, contraceptive pill and preventative procedures available if fun is all you're after. Parenting is not for everyone, and if you know you fall into that category you owe it to humanity to make better decisions in that respect. It's probably best to hold off bringing a child into this world if there are obvious challenges like addictions or homelessness. But hey, needs must and shit happens. Not even I can hold back the destiny of a selfie-obsessed generation.

If like the 'Immaculate Conception' you seemingly had no other options available but to have a child, understand that it takes a village to raise a '**natural human child**'. Your lifestyle has no option but to change because children come to remind you about what's really important (if anyone tells you otherwise take it with a pinch of salt). You can kiss sleep and anything of material importance goodbye. Perhaps before, you could spontaneously go on a holiday to Ibiza and party till the wee hours of the morning. Now, you have to make arrangements for childcare and if you have a child with different or particular needs, prepare for that in advance. If you can afford a 24-hour nanny, good for you, but you might miss out on key bonding and development phases in your child's life. When they're older you might get a reprieve, but that depends on the child, how they were raised and the state of the global economy.

Children are part of humanity's heritage (legacy) because they don't actually belong to you or the state. Through you the Prime Creator paves the way for another unique human experience and the gene pool for the next generation. When they are of age they have a right to self-determination.

CHAPTER FOUR

EGO? WHAT EGO?

"The ego is nothing other than the focus of conscious attention."

Alan Watts

This chapter was definitely inspired by an interaction with a very interesting gentleman I attracted into my life. He played a very delicate game with me where, when he wanted something from me I was incredible, a genius, very beautiful and a rock star (all very true of course). When I wanted something in return I went down a notch and became difficult, less incredible, and not as smart as expected, great but nothing without him. It was so subtle that if I blinked I'd have missed this controlling aspect of his personality. His ego was so self-righteous that if you had a puny sense of self you'd fall for his antics and begin to question your behaviour. In hindsight, it was an illusionary game devised by somebody up there with a sense of humour to test my mettle. He wasn't a bad person our egos were at loggerheads. In fact, he was a catalyst in getting the whole writing project started and remains a very dear person to me. My ego was not buying what he was selling and I had to learn to stand up for myself. He most likely had to update his belief systems and prejudices concerning me. His need for control showed me that he felt powerless around me and had to contain it the only way he knew, by using age, displays of wealth, connections and achievement. If you've ever met someone with a huge ego the rest of the chapter is totally fun to sink your teeth into.

The **Oxford Dictionary defines the ego as a person's sense of self-esteem or self-importance**. In psychoanalysis, the ego is defined as the part of the mind that mediates between the conscious and unconscious and is responsible for reality testing and a sense of personal identity. In metaphysics the ego is described as the conscious thinking subject. From my perspective, which is a fusion of psychoanalysis and metaphysics, **the ego** is **a magical lens, mask and filter** through which one can experience the idea of physical reality. **It is your physical consciousness or personality mind**.

A seismic ego is just a very outdated or misplaced sense of self, much like Mr. Toad of Toad Hall in Wind in the

The Learning Years

The learning years feels like the hardest years to go through in life. Your friends are busy doing something fantastic while you remain stagnant in the same place, unmoved and seemingly apathetic about the goings-on around you. Major breakthroughs in your life that should be celebrated appear minuscule in comparison to your neighbours.

Their constant babble about every single victory puts a strain on you and sows the seeds of doubt in your well-structured life. You begin to wonder if you are genuinely happy for them, or behind that tight-lipped smile is brooding jealousy. Your supplications to the unknown become fervent, as you demand to know your life path. You veer off course. Delayed gratification is no longer your catchphrase. Good sense walks out and your hunger for NOW intensifies.

The learning years feels like the hardest years to go through in life. You slow down at bends and give way to others. Other times you accelerate on motorways, the wind in your hair, speed at your feet, life in your clasp and forgetting that these moments will pass.

The earning years follow the learning years though at times there will be an over lap. Times when you feel frustrated and inactive, these are to be cherished and adored. For life is swift and short you'll never get back the time you lost when you were supposed to be learning.

Le Feebs

Willows if you've read it. Toad is the wealthy occupant and owner of Toad Hall and is able to indulge in his impulsive desires; however, he is very narcissistic and self-centred. There's nothing inherently wrong with a strong sense of self, but if your ego thinks you're better than another human being, conscious life or someone or something is beneath you, then you have a very misplaced ego or you have only developed the masculine aspects of your being and not the feminine side. Balancing your masculine and feminine traits alone will keep your ego at bay. Most men in society tend to have a huge sense of self as the masculine is more revered than the feminine in our current culture, but a misinformed ego is no respecter of gender. There are countless women with inflated egos too.

It's imperative to have your own mind and learn to filter out the conditioning from your parents and society at large. It's surprising how much we take as fact without questioning whether this is true for us or not. Women are trained to stay on their knees because those that learn to stand on their own ask too many questions, are labelled feminists and threaten the fragile masculine ego. I'm optimistic you've learned by now, that **there are no gender roles; only the ones defined and chosen by YOU**. If you are to start taking control of your life, you must start being responsible for what your magical lens picks up. Again, it's what you allow and what you don't allow that determines and colours your experiences. Although Mr. Toad had a misplaced sense of self, he remains one my favourite fictional characters as he is loveable and has a heart of gold much like my catalyst.

The human body is like your own enchanted piece of the Earth and the ego-mind, its ruler. Its workings are mysterious, complicated and simple and clear all at the same time. Your beliefs, thoughts, feelings and desires are the ego's subjects and only by treating them with grace and endearment will your kingdom flourish. From religion to science, Freud to Jung and new age mantras, in recent times, the ego has been assigned a bad reputation when in fact it was simply doing its job. Being so focused by the ego, we conveniently forget that life is not confined to just what we can see, hear, touch, taste and smell. There's so much more to it.

I would like to think that most of us no longer buy into the supposed sexual repression and crucifixion of the ego mind and our desires anymore. Surely what is making most of us cranky are the unfulfilled desires we've talked ourselves out of, due to some of the choices made. We keep hampering our desires, set restrictive conditions and demand that a deity take responsibility for the lack of indecision and inaction on our part. Let's face it, in this dimension and current time frame, scientists, psychologists and psychoanalysts don't understand our supernatural purpose any more than religious figureheads do and yet we all get caught up with the minute details and buy into their various complicated methods we don't half believe. **Countless studies with placebos have found that any method works as long as you believe**

in it, though practitioners of one will never agree that other methods, roads and paths work too.

The ego is therefore all about the physical world and its trappings. It is to keep you 100% focused in physical reality. If it wasn't here we would have to plug ourselves in and out of the physical world like Neo and Morpheus did in The Matrix (I don't know about you but I'd rather not do that on a daily basis).

Your primary beliefs then feed the ego mind. They tell it how to act, react and respond based on the data given to it, as illustrated in Figure 3.

Figure 3

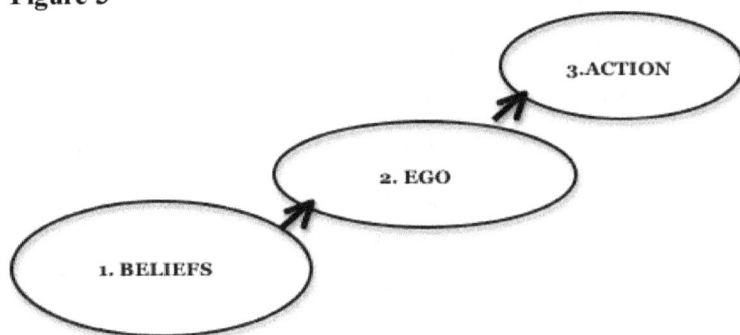

The ego mind can also be made to feel unworthy if it's fed consistently malignant information. The ego like everything else is a tool that can be tuned for positive experiences or negative ones. It all depends on YOU. You are the gatekeeper. It's your domain and you have all the choice and free will backing whatever decision you make.

Most of us never pay attention to what we feed our personality mind until we go from the frying pan into the fire. Your ego's reaction in the face of adversity is one of the most effective ways that your Higher Self can highlight to you that there is something inherently wrong with your belief structure. The ego can also rear its head during religious, scientific, political and ideological debates when you watch them go at each other about whose God is superior or whose ideology is more powerful and important.

What you buy into concerning your abilities, culture, religion, relationships, people, society, and politics is all played out by your ego personality mind. You can change how your ego mind operates, if you change your core beliefs concerning the areas in your life you want to transform. The ego's job is not to dictate how to live your life. The 'Higher Self YOU' is in charge of your day-to-day and the ego mind is its sceptre. We are unconscious to this fact because, 'the greatest power requires the lightest touch'.

Your Higher Self uses tact, hints, and the obvious to talk to you and get your attention. This comes in the form of intuition, synchronicities and serendipities. If you recall, I was after a 'burning bush', an illuminated sign under the TDK advertisement in the northwestern corner between Shaftsbury Avenue and Glasshouse Street. In hindsight the simplest solution was to start writing because I frequented the British library from Monday to Friday like I was on their payroll. The clues were there the whole time and I was oblivious to it.

The reason why meditation is such a big deal is because our minds are cluttered with a whole bunch of stuff that is irrelevant on closer inspection that hinders our communication with the Higher Self. If you're attracted to meditation as a process to calm the mind, do it. If you're not, try something else. It's pointless wasting a lot of time, money and effort on a process you don't enjoy. You end up creating more stress and resentment, rendering the whole process futile. Personally meditation was fun whilst the urge to do it was strong, but it wasn't a process I was passionate about, so I let it go and found joy in reading the Daily Mail (DM) comments section and dancing to Afrobeats for thirty minutes every day. You won't believe it, but the DM gave me more book material than 30 minutes of meditation. Who knows maybe at some point in my journey I will find meditation attractive and pursue it again.

As a collective we often place too much strain on the ego mind wanting it to be in charge of our daily lives when it's not in the job description. We have gotten extremely smart at treating symptoms (feelings & actions) with chemicals that we have become mentally idle and have let the ego mind take the reins. We are not dealing with the obvious, that is to say we need a 'conscious revolution', a shake-up of our collective consciousness. Our society is too focused on restricting and containing our actions but fail to look at the root cause. If we believed better, we would act accordingly. You can't tell a killer not to kill, unless he genuinely believes it's wrong to kill.

The belief changes behaviour and not the other way round. When someone suffers from depression we are very quick to prescribe lithium. That person is evidently suffering from chronic feelings of unworthiness and is crying out for help. But since science isn't convinced yet of our divine nature and the existence of a higher force, lithium it is. It is time to shine the light on the questionable nature of some our cultural expressions.

The other day, I read about the International Criminal Court's (ICC) investigation into unlawful killing of civilians during the 2003 Iraq war, I found myself chuckling at this contradiction. My interest in politics is minimal at best, although the whole set up is a great reflection of the human condition right now: MAJOR CONFUSION! We can change it if we want to, but as emotionally lethargic as we are, or as I read somewhere the other day 'the coma of delusion' we clothe ourselves in, the pace of change might take some time. As a society that supposedly shuns violence we are truly adept at masking our flaws with semantics. We are either opposed to violence or not. When violence becomes acceptable in some instances, the lines begin to blur. Who sets the rules for acceptable death and who is judiciously allowed to carry out lawful killing?

We all share the blame collectively as we are our governments. No one is looking into why we have such a distorted view of basic fundamental truths. Why is violence our first response when we feel powerless? If we all cooperatively agreed to discard violent behaviour and language, culled the use of excessive force from our society, what kind of world would we inhabit? Our egos are blinded with self-righteousness and have become heavily invested in disempowerment and playing the victim. The matrix is running us and not the other way round.

With no first-hand experience in domestic violence in this incarnation, I have witnessed many close friends and family members go through it. It is the most heartbreaking encounter to watch your loved ones go through. There are various reasons why both men and women stay in abusive relationships. A truly balanced mind can walk away from anything that proves harmful and no longer serves them. However, most tend to linger in unhealthy relationships due to feelings of unworthiness primarily. As a firm believer in the '**Law of Correspondence**': 'as within so without, as above, so below', one has to take a step back and say what beliefs do I have about myself that will make me entertain or reflect an abusive lover?

Assuming a man essentially believes women are the weaker sex; it's the ego's job as the filter to find all the evidence that supports this belief. If it ever comes across anything contrary to that idea, it may result in an outrage that shuts down your reasoning abilities. Some men resort to violence because somewhere along the line they've bought into the idea that it is right to physically violate another human being when you feel powerless. Coupled with the idea of thinking that women are weak and violence is acceptable results in physical or verbal abuse.

Equally the partner on the receiving end is not as innocent as society will have us believe. Don't be too quick to label and judge the abuser, somewhere along the lines they have also been victims. They say *'hurt people, hurt people'* and that is true of abusers. To attract or accept abusive behaviour is also indicative that you have bought into the same belief system as the abuser and that one's dominance or power is asserted through violence. You are also tolerating the abuse because of the love and attention you hope to get from them. Any form of attention is better than no attention at all; in his anger at least you can feel his presence with you. These two are a perfect match in beliefs but express them differently. They both feel powerless in their lives and act it out differently.

This is an oversimplification of a very sensitive issue as there might be other hidden intentions and beliefs working here too. Abuse comes in many forms and this example focuses on physical abuse. A belief in a concept has unlimited permutations. Depending on both the woman and man's cultural and religious beliefs about men being the primary provider and the head of the house, in conjunction with fear based beliefs about money, a woman may be inclined to stay;

in order to provide a roof over her children's head and childcare as it's challenging being a single parent. It may also be an issue of one's culture, immigration status, addictions and or employability. Other times it's an emotional purpose of trying to be the saviour and feeling needed. It's very easy to get lost in someone else's challenges and think you can solve it for them, believing your love is enough for the both of you.

They may also have been conditioned by society to believe the notion that men were more important than women and without men, women were nothing. Most of us have also bought into erroneous beliefs that relationships are extremely hard work and that enduring these challenges is the test of true love. Together all these intentions and agendas form the structure of the ego's mind at play in this domestic drama pitting us against one another. Individuals have the potential of being so disagreeable you want to eliminate them or so magnificent you want to be with them forever.

They say every conversation you have with others, is really a conversation with yourself. You use your interaction with others as a mirror for what's going on with you. People also come into your life to show you love when you need it the most. Other times it's to propel you unto the next phase of your life journey. If you have an unhealthy belief structure, you will gravitate to or bring out these hidden beliefs in others. If you have chosen to participate in an abusive relationship, the question is why are you punishing yourself? What are you trying to teach yourself that requires violence and mental ridicule? When you finally appreciate that there is not a person or thing responsible for your emotional balance but yourself, you will stop holding others to an impossible standard.

If you or anyone you know is going through something similar to what I described, please seek help from a registered professional who handles abuse. Domestic violence/abuse is not gender specific. Trying to extract a healthy relationship from an unacceptable source is counterproductive. When there's violence involved, anything can provoke it. Always leave imminent danger first then delve into your mind. **Remember the onus is not on the other person to change, but for you to change because you cannot change the reflection in the mirror until you change.**

For women, our emotional mind is our logical guidance system. If something doesn't feel or sit right with you, please don't second-guess yourself or say 'I'm just being crazy'. This is probably one of the most destroying beliefs the female psyche has bought into. Women have certain cerebral connections men lack. It's nothing new that the female brain is wired differently to a man's. This is to enhance the connection between the mother and child before and after childbirth. We are incubators and life givers for goodness sake. Stop letting others; especially some men talk you out of very valid emotions and feelings. Men don't second-guess their decisions so why should you at any point distrust a feeling of unease. I'd suggest walking away from heated discussions and take time out to process whatever feedback your guidance system is telling you then come back and articulate it if you so desire or not. Women are fantastic and it's high time they started acting like the goddesses they were created to be. For men, if something sounds illogical to your reasoning mind, pay attention to it and take action.

The greatest act of love is to teach self-love, self-respect and self-worth. It's about extending the level of care; love and concern that you expect to receive from others to yourself. Staying only reinforces an abusive behaviour and belief system. Every relationship serves a purpose and that purpose is to reflect to everyone in it what he or she needs to understand to become more of their **divine natural selves**. Ideally they are used to explore and flag anything that feels out of place with your preferences. You are made stronger when your weaknesses are tested and exposed. If you don't pay attention and heed the lessons, the same relationship will keep coming back in different packages but with the same theme.

I understand the need for validation from someone else. I was so desperate for love and wanted to be ravished and swept off my feet so badly that I was quick to label every experience with any Tom, Dick and Harry as love, when they were purely carnal in nature. It wasn't until recently that I realised I had some very flawed definitions of love that were in dire need of a makeover. I was settling for crumbs when I had access to unconditional love within. I held a very distorted view of what love entailed and thankfully I discovered that love is not complicated; it's straightforward, challenging but not painful, self-assured but selfless. Until you're open to love in this way, it's very much a foreign concept. When you're great within yourself, you're going to attract so much amazing energy because you emit love and balance. You no longer need another human being to fill a hole created by your outdated beliefs and unfulfilled desires. You're focused on being happy with yourself no matter what and you know that you're more than enough as a self-sufficient loving being who brings a lot to the table.

In the grand scheme of things, a relationship is not the 'Holy Grail' they want us to believe it is. You have to be deluded if you think being Instagram and Facebook official is an achievement. I understand the ego inflation aspect it gives you to parade this union on social media, but is that all there is to you? Is the peak of your existence your ability to attract a partner and generate 100 plus likes? Romantic love is not more important than the love you share with your family, friends and most importantly yourself. Your family and friends are your soul mates first before any other.

There's more to love than looks and status and your criteria for a partner in all aspects of your life should evolve if you want an improvement in that field. Aim for respect, love, peace, happiness, fun, explorations, discussions, flexibility, and space to grow and discover your true nature. If it's status you're after, you'll have more fun and freedom creating it for yourself instead of depending on someone. Women are co-leaders and co-providers too. Refer back to the 'Law of Gender** and see how both genders work together harmoniously in order to manifest and create life in the Universe.

I've witnessed many marriages come under strain with women giving up their earning power because some religious book said so or society's warped view validates this. The male and female energy, both **co-exist, co-create** and **co-lead**. YOU ARE CO-EQUALS! Unity and harmony is the key. Some women prefer to lead at home; others prefer to lead from work. It's up to you as a woman and a couple to decide what works for you. Some men are opting to be stay at home husbands and fathers these days because let's face it; if the woman earns more, it makes no financial sense for her to give up her career.

There would be no male without female and no female without male. The Prime Creator is egalitarian by nature. I certainly refuse to believe that I chose to incarnate as a woman to have anyone let alone a man rule over me. Because of the nature of free will, no relationship is guaranteed. People change their minds regularly and often and why not? You better have your own passions and hobbies going on, instead of making another person your project. **I can't stress this enough, the key to success lies in the relationship you have with yourself**, as that is your point of connection to the outside world. Apart from that anything goes. Don't leave it to other people to take care of you. There's nothing like living your passion and knowing that everything you have came from All That Is through you and no one else and passing that belief on to your children. All partnerships and relationships are 100:100 not 50:50. Anything less than putting in your whole self is skewed and is definitely a red flag. I'm not talking about having joint accounts. I'm not sold on that to be honest. I'm talking about the kind of union where partner A takes 100% responsibility for their emotional state; and partner B does the same. Together A + B can consciously have a balanced, happy and healthy relationship.

Anything that makes you feel or act out of your integrity or comes up with some resistance is the area in your life that relationship is forcing you to work on. Contrast is good in any relationship; it helps you eradicate the unconscious resistance hindering your joy and excitement in any venture. It all depends on how you look at it. I always say look for how someone resolves conflict (now that I'm single and emotionally available I seem to have lost the art of a good quarrel *sigh*). Are they manipulative, patronising, condescending, fair, balanced, apologetic, understanding, or do they tend to have public outbursts? Do they take steps to ensure it doesn't happen again? Or do they retreat and aim to please you so will say anything to make the conflict disappear in the short term? You're after someone's emotional maturity here. Someone who is comfortable in their own skin, who says what they mean and means what they say and is very self-aware. You also want someone with the same values in the same order of priority and the same definitions. Our inability to identify what we want and thus qualify the people around us is usually what breaks our hearts.

If your life varies from what you say you ideally want, there's something amiss with your beliefs or you're playing catch up to it like I was. It doesn't mean there's something wrong with you; it just means you're giving your power away in the present moment. Life is NOW and placing your happiness on some arbitrary point in the future and instead of being happy now is looking for love in all the wrong places. What if this future you crave never shows up?

Marriage and long-term relationships like most things are not for everyone. But only come to this conclusion from an informed stance, not from someone else's fears and mishaps. Don't get caught up in the excitement of a proposal and the validation of 2-carat, D-flawless, Royal Asscher Cut diamond ring (if you don't believe me ask Frodo Baggins about the power of the ring). Some have been very successful with marriage; so you'll never know for sure until you've tried this one: just make sure the odds or self-awareness are stacked in your favour.

There's no such thing as a perfect person or situation, however that doesn't absolve you of the responsibility of distancing or cutting yourself off from situations that are not healthy. If you're not the right person for them, they are not the right person for you either. Violence is obviously a no-no.

If someone you love is repeatedly disrespectful and you don't speak up and correct it, that's not love. You are just sending out a very clear message that you don't value your wellbeing, because your actions (energy in motion) prove this. You are refusing to accept the reality and projecting your preferred version of events on them. It's like watching a three-year-old disrespect an adult and no one corrects and transforms that behaviour immediately. All parties witnessing it have taught the three-year-old that it is acceptable to behave like this. Correction and punishment are two different things not to be confused. Correction is the love transformation, whilst punishment has nothing to do with love. Punishment is your ego's way of getting even or your own back.

It is important not to underestimate the ego mind and give it the respect it deserves. The ego is so great at what it does; it's almost hard to believe it exists as an aide and not as your true nature. It's easy to point fingers at someone and label him or her evil, bad, unworthy or scum. It's more psychologically challenging to take a step back and say, this is not who they are, they must have bought into a belief which doesn't help them. Why do they feel powerless and how am I playing a part in this? In their moment of insanity how do I effect change in them? Sometimes these questions will cause us to walk away from those we love for a time until both parties figure out what they want and thus determine what method of interaction is acceptable for them.

By using regular disagreements and conflicts, we can get in touch with some of our outdated definitions concerning race, religion, society and science. **How do you know if it's your ego mind doing the talking or your Goddess self? Is it coming from a place of love or fear? Do you have to put yourself or anyone down in the process?** If it's coming from a place of Love, it's your Higher Self/God Nature talking. Anything else is your ego mind *'throwing shade'* (urban word for picking out one's flaws in a derogatory manner, most likely a euphemism for schadenfreude don't quote me).

One of the many ways to tune your ego to a desired outcome is to have a physical contract with it. When I stumbled upon this fact I was ecstatic and thus keen to spread the word. As the ego mind is your conscious personality mind, it has successfully navigated you into this present moment; hence your old belief system must be honoured. Everything it has done until now, has been done out of love for you albeit misinformed. The ego is all about the physical world and physical business. It's smart to negotiate a fair deal with your ego, so you do not self-sabotage. Be open, brutally honest and flexible with your agreement because the ego is all about winning. Use your imagination and full disclosure so your ego doesn't feel tricked. Be precise and gentle. Do not rush the process, as that will paradoxically delay your goals and manifestations. As the most important thing in your life, it is essential to engage your conscious mind fully. Make deals with your ego that let you stretch some of your belief systems in increments as this enables you to find a relative balance point.

I should point out that as you change your underlying beliefs, your personality filter will also change, sometimes faster than you can imagine. Believe me when I say you literally change moment-by-moment as new information comes to your body consciousness. What was previously acceptable to your personality mind will no longer be or feel acceptable. Things that use to piss you off will no longer be an issue. When you're finally being honest, available and living in line with your values, your ego will flag anything that doesn't belong in your new belief framework and will find various ways to get your attention in order to get you to align with your new values.

I found out that as my ego changed and took on new empowering beliefs I was playing catch up to it. Even when I was receiving information via actions and words that should rightly change my feelings and trust levels; I proceeded blindly hoping that my positive feelings and affirmations alone will carry the situation. Stop rejecting the information your senses are receiving loud and clear and accept it for what it is.

I also discovered that finding out what your new and improved personality mind was trying to communicate was not very straightforward and easy to comprehend in the beginning. I recommend stipulating ease and simplicity in your ego contract otherwise you may end up spending weeks, months and years instead of days adjusting to your new and improved outlook. However, when the penny finally drops and you get that eureka moment, it's the most liberating feeling ever. Over time, your communication and alignment with your fabulous ego will feel easier, lighter and the personality mind will want to feel the burden lifted off its shoulders. If an ego contract appeals to you do it, if it sounds ridiculous, leave it alone, as it's clearly a process not for you.

The Take Away...

- The ego is the lens you use to filter all life experiences.
- The ego mind is not your true mind; it's just your personality mind and personalities can change.
- Your lens gets its data from your beliefs; hence you must change your beliefs before your ego/personality changes.
- Someone with an inflated ego is a misinformed person, not a bad person.
- You cannot save anyone but yourself; the responsibility is on the individuals to save themselves. No one can do the mental and emotional work on anyone's behalf. All you can do is provide them with the unconditional loving space so they can reach out and become better in their actions. Blame this flawed premise on saving others on religion.
- Balance the masculine and feminine energy within to keep the ego at bay and working for your good.
- Draw out a contract with your ego (or not) and negotiate something that ensures it wins from the arrangement too.

This Too Shall Pass

*In my moment of great splendour,
it will pass.
In my flashes of great melancholy,
this too, will pass.
In my lover's embrace,
I am reminded that this joyous
twinkle will unquestionably pass.
Beaming with laughter and radiating beauty
I recall that, 'aha' this too, will pass*

*As I wake up in agony and heartbroken
I hear a whisper, soft and clairvoyant
Saying, "this, too, will pass".
When all seems lost, and my worst fears are realised.
Loneliness awaits me
and sorrow overtakes me
that too, will certainly pass.*

*At my weakest and at my strongest
It shall surely, pass.
Spending time with friends, loved ones and family members,
is but a second away from history.
Life waits for no one and,
Time is only generous to those who value it*

*Hence I attempt to make the most of every emotion,
At times I fail, but the gift of time and second, third and fourth
chances prevail.
Life is fleeting and Henley's notion only a fantasy.
I vow to maximise my utility in the positive sense,
Knowing that this epiphany shall surely PASS!*

Le Feebs

CHAPTER FIVE

THE EMOTIONAL ALCHEMIST

"We now understand that higher-level of thinking is more likely to occur in the brain of a student who is emotionally secure than in the brain of a student, who is scared, upset, anxious or stressed."

Mawhinney & Sagan

When you're going through stressful times, it's very easy to forget that everything has an end. Be it one day, one week, one month or one year whatever you're defining as stressful has an end if you decide that it should. The world around us plays a large part in how our inner world develops and is allowed to express itself. Your emotions are an indicator of what's going on around you and what is active in your vibrational reality. If your happiness is tied to people or things happening around you, you might find yourself waiting a long time to be truly happy because there's bound to be something or someone who is likely to piss you off on a daily basis.

One of the few borrowed mantras I have on a loop in my head is *'circumstances don't matter, only state of being'*. In other words, as creators, our state of being is the materialising factor in our reality not circumstances. Matter is merely a grouping of atoms composed of electrons constantly vibrating. Everything on our planet and Universe is made out of vibrating atoms and crystallised matter (refer back to **Law of Vibration**). Your state of being causes the non-physical to become physical because if you are consistently happy and confident in certain aspects of your life, those aspects will eventually reflect all your desires in that area (**Law of Attraction**). Matter bends to the human will and intent.

In the words of my fictional BFF (best friend forever) Albus Dumbledore, *'happiness can be found in the darkest of times, if only one remembers to turn on the light'*. The aspects of the vibrating matter you focus on is what determines how your reality will unfold. In plain English, everything has the potential to be great or disappointing depending on your focus. For example, if your car breaks down in the middle of nowhere and you have an important appointment to get to, you're better off thinking 'it must be a sign for me to slow down', or 'I'm probably being prevented from an inconvenience ahead'. Rather than to say things like 'typical, always happens to me' and roll your eyes in disdain. By not appreciating it from that viewpoint of love and care, you create emotional resistance to the situation and will most likely continue to attract more breakdowns and unwanted illusions into your reality that day. It's where statements like *bad luck comes in threes* stem from. You have to accept the break down and believe that it's exactly what needed to happen in that moment. It is a great vantage point for you to bless what is and objectively say, 'what productive thing can I learn about myself, and life from this situation?' Oh and don't forget to call the AA while you're at it.

Alternatively, you can spend a lot of time examining the infinite causes and effects that brought about breakdown-gate, what events affected your timing to precisely place you in synchronicity with the faulty car? Who was the last person to use it? How did they come by it? What caused the breakdown? When was it last serviced? What affected your mental state of being to make you to react the way you did? What was the uncaused first cause of breakdown-gate and so on and so forth? Through a negative belief-filter one might even come to a ridiculous, albeit valid conclusion like, that would have never happened to them if they were never born. I've met a number of people who use this logic whenever something unwanted happens to them. On a surface level, it was just a car that broke down. It has no inherent meaning till you assign one to it. Giving meaning to matter is what bends it to your will.

We gravitate to a lot of processes, ideologies, people, and relationships because challenges of self-worth and external approval plague many of us throughout our lives. After going through some of these processes we emerge more confident and sure of our capabilities, though this isn't always the case. Life is not challenge-free; it's designed this way to keep us engaged, and forces us to delve deeper and remember who we are and connect to the creative loving source within. I'm not a firm believer in too many mantras, strange methods and processes because it begins to contradict a belief that everything works out for your good, no matter what. I believe we live in a charmed Universe and it works very well on its own without interference. Forgetting this will have you looking for even more methods and processes that never really work because Mother Nature and our own nature work best when left alone in complete trust of the benevolence of Creation itself. Nature doesn't use methods; it works because it is designed to work. If jumping from process to process, job to job or relationship to relationship is exciting and is an expression of joy for you then by all means you have my blessing.

Ideally, our parents and the adults in society would possess the necessary tools to equip us to deal with life, but most of them, never took the time out to find some of the answers to life's questions before settling down and starting a family (forever putting the cart before the horse). We inherit so many of our emotional tools from our parents, family, friends and our environment. If they displayed a lot of aggression to you and nothing else you might go around thinking rage and aggression is the modus operandi when communicating with others, because let's face it emotions are contagious. I've had to teach myself how to handle a lot of the feelings that bubble up inside when something unpleasant occurs. **Emotional literacy and intelligence is one of the most important things to wrap your head around as it spells balance and makes life feel much easier and lighter.** Having feelings does not translate into emotional intelligence and maturity. We all have feelings; it doesn't mean we know what to do with them when they show up. When you're emotionally intelligent you become superconductive to all good things around you, because you possess the tools to handle them. You understand that no one does anything to you emotionally you do it to yourself. You are able to give emotional meaning and significance to another person's actions and it's completely your choice in deciding how to respond.

One of the best African proverbs I encountered recently was *'if you answer a mad man, you look like colleagues'*. A dear friend once told me that the best way to handle an unwanted situation was to imagine wearing a red jacket and someone coming up to you shouting 'I FUCKING HATE GREEN JACKETS!' This statement obviously has nothing to do with you or your red jacket. The most logical thing to do in that situation is to walk away and smile in amazement. Trying to engage or berate them in their anger is what this proverb beautifully outlines. The red jacket represents your true self; most of the time people don't recognise that they are wearing red jackets, because they haven't taken the time out to find out that they are red instead of green. By reacting to the insanity of the green jacket statement you begin to play someone else's game instead of yours.

A good response usually means walking away or resolving it in a peaceful way. Your ability to respond instead of reacting is usually a sign of development, stability and balance in an individual. The proverb '*a clear conscience fears no accusations*' means that when you know what your true intentions are in any situation, when something goes seemingly wrong you are not so easily lead of your path of truth. A reaction implies that you are easily swayed by circumstances and your definition of who you are is unstable and insecure. No man has achieved anything by reacting from a place of fear and insecurity in the face of adversity.

My coping mechanism for daily life challenges is a technique I borrowed from Jerry and Esther Hicks. I am definitely still adjusting to this method. At the core of this is the **Law of Relativity**. To make myself feel better, when things don't quite work out, I work myself up an ingenious emotional scale (one of the few processes I condone) devised by the Hicks from their book "Ask and It is Given", pg. 114. The scale goes up from powerlessness, anger, blame and optimism all the way up to joy and empowerment. Anything towards the top of emotional scare is a state of being with little to zero mental resistance.

If we take a look at the guidance scale we can see that the top five: joy, passion, enthusiasm, positive expectation and optimism are the positive creative forces and they align all good things to you, whilst the bottom five: revenge, hatred, jealousy, insecurity and fear attract all the negative creative forces and energy to you. It's a great way to use **Law of Relativity** and the **Law of Attraction** to your advantage.

For a long time, I was taught to frown on boredom, when in fact it is a great place to be in comparison to other low vibration resistant thoughts. The scale gives pessimism a new light in comparison to disappointment. It's also evident that you can't stay in hope for too long as it has an element of doubt attached to the outcome. Certainly every time I express hope, I inadvertently say I know this won't work out but I challenge you to prove me wrong. It's much more effective and productive to remain optimistic than hopeful (and to think most of the causes and foundations are grounded in hope rather enthusiasm or passion, we really have a long way to go as humanity).

By the end of it, I am certain you'll come to appreciate every person and event as gold dust to a better feeling place. Dare I say it you might even paint the town red when chaos ensues because you know you'll be in a better state of being after it's over.

So here's how to use it: If like me a job you want goes amiss, your attention to the loss will cause you great despair. You have the option of a better feeling thought from a place of insecurity/guilt at (**21**) like 'maybe I'm not good enough for the job' to anger (**17**) such as 'oh for crying out loud why didn't I get the bloody job?' That gives you a little relief.

Abraham Hicks Emotional Guidance Scale

1.	Joy/Appreciation/Empowerment/Freedom/Unconditional Love
2.	Passion
3.	Enthusiasm/Eagerness/Happiness
4.	Positive Expectation/Belief
5.	Optimism
6.	Hopefulness
7.	Contentment
8.	Boredom
9.	Pessimism
10.	Frustration/Irritation/Impatience
11.	Overwhelming
12.	Disappointment
13.	Doubt
14.	Worry
15.	Blame
16.	Discouragement
17.	Anger
18.	Revenge
19.	Hatred/Rage
20.	Jealousy
21.	Insecurity/Guilt/Unworthiness
22.	Fear/Grief/Depression/Despair/Powerlessness

As you gradually work your way up you might even think, 'I can't believe I trusted them to give me a job, I'm a little disappointed'. This calls you up from anger (17) to disappointment (12). Compassion and hopefulness (6) are exercised when you think 'I've equally let others down in the past' and you begin to lighten up a little bit. Clemency comes in when you consider that, you've lied to others in the past when you didn't think they could handle the truth. Then you think, 'I can't even remember why I'm upset about this job it was clearly not meant for me'. Enthusiasm (3) says 'why am I making a big deal out of this? I trust in the process and the benevolence of the Universe, what is meant to be for me will be.'

This process used over time will get you back faster into a joyous and attractive state of being and will eventually become unconscious in your make up. Depending on the issue it might take some years, months, weeks or days. I will suggest not rushing through it so you truly and honestly transmute the issue, let it go and leave it in the past. I encourage you to write this down, as every emotional state is valid and true and must be acknowledged and respected. It's okay to feel fear and anger, just learn to reach for a better feeling thought, like disappointment to relieve you of mental stress and emotional pain. Like an alchemist continue to convert the emotions and feelings up the scale till you neutralise the situation and express golden unconditional love and joy.

Over time you will no longer require people and circumstances to bend to your will. You'll realise that there really isn't a source of negativity or evil, just unconditional love, allowed or disallowed by your beliefs, thoughts and feelings. You receive everything you want be it good or bad in the presence or absence of doubt and resistance.

You don't necessarily have to use the scale like I have outlined. Find out what works best for your personality and temperament. Do it with friends, family, or someone you can trust. Ensure whoever you're doing it with is in a better or higher emotional state than you (**Law of Sympathetic Resonance**). If you're angry, let them call you up to a place of pessimism or hope. If you're disappointed and your friend is also disappointed, the whole situation will feel much worse than it needs to. I tend to do it with my imaginary friends and the many voices in my head and some trusted loved ones. Some learn best with a hard line approach. I prefer a mixture of soft and hard depending on the issue I'm transmuting. Have fun with how you get over your issues as long as you let them go in the end.

LOVE

What is love?
Is love when there are butterflies in your stomach?
Is love when the heart grows fonder?
Is love just a verbal ritual?

Does love need an action to amplify the feeling?
Does love include unmerited favour?
Can love be expressed on paper?
Can it be justified by the flow of the ink?
Can love be the verb or the pronoun?

Is it found in the simile or the metaphor?
Is love when the sun shines?
Is love when the trees grow?
Is it love when we see yet another day?

Can love be the exuberance of life?
Can love be found in a physical state?
Can love be discovered in beauty or is beauty discovered in love?

Would you say love is in the rising of the sun, the air we breathe, our shelter and food?
Would you say love can only be depicted by the author and finisher of life? Or
Perhaps love is contained within the mouth that created it all

Le Feebs

CHAPTER SIX

WHEN LIMITS PROVE USEFUL

'...In the happy and joyous journey to me I discover I am god. The power to do whatever I want is within me. Nobody can stop me. I am an eternal, limitless being. The limits I experience are those I choose. The external gods I experience are ones that I choose to believe in and give power to...'

Le Feebs

Above is an excerpt from a poem I wrote concerning the self-imposed limits of my journey to self- discovery from broader perspective. In my opinion, it totally sums up what this book is about. Fundamentally, everything we experience is by choice. At times, we conveniently forget that we are unlimited spiritual beings and the limits experienced are dictated by the belief systems we buy into and the choices we make. Absolutely everything can be whittled down to a spiritual experience because *experience* is the name of the game.

Limits are choices and a Universe without choice is unimaginable. The choices we make come fully loaded with energy, which has an effect when expressed in the illusionary world we inhabit. By **Merriam Webster's definition, the word *limit* means something that bounds, restrains or confines**. Without boundaries how will you identify your destination, location and frequency? Imagine getting off the plane at Heathrow and not being able to find central London, because it had not been defined and confined within the British Isles. How would you even board a plane with no destination in mind? It's important to have a geographical location, a map to point out where North, South, East and West are. Destination points need to be identifiable, confined, labelled and differentiated.

On an emotional level, boundaries help you resist the urge to bend to someone's will. They form a framework, which allows you to create a strong Earth identity of what you stand for and what you willing to put up with. It also helps others identify if you're on the same page for a relationship, business venture or a cause. Limits are an expressive tool. They don't affect who you are just the contents and measure of your experience. Your value to Creation is bigger than any boundary or restraint you set. See! The advantages of limits are endless and we're only on the second page of the chapter.

With the success of 'The Secret', the word limit has become a faux pas in our lexicon, because everyone seems to be after unlimited wealth. The decision to experience unlimited wealth is a boundary, a choice and thus a limit in itself as you have excluded all limited options and permutation in Creation. By definition then, there are no inherent negative connotations with limits, except the ones we impose on it. Limits are useful if you want to set certain parameters for your human experience, i.e. get married, buy a house, become a bum, stay away from drugs or become a senior executive at a Fortune 500 company. Because they are self-imposed, they are also adjustable.

In calculus (which I took for 2 years in undergrad and I am shocked I'm using it for something), limits are used to define an integer (a whole number), or a destination point in a functional equation. Stay with my glorious attempt at sounding über intelligent for a minute. The term 'functional equation' usually refers to algebraic equations that cannot be reduced to simpler equations like **6x + 2 = 14**, where **x = 2**, as there are too many variables. "**6x + 2 = 14**" also simplifies to "**3x + 1 = 7**" (FYI). In this example (**x**) is the only variable to consider. If you add another variable (**y**) to the equation, i.e. **6x +2y = 14**, though not difficult to solve, starts to complicate things. A functional equation in calculus is therefore used to find solutions to complex equations where the variables can include, **(x), (y) or (z),** or the solutions to the equation are **indeterminate (0/0)** or the answer is

infinite (∞). The indeterminate and infinite do have values; we just don't know what they are mathematically but they help us simplify the unknown and the equation.

There are all sorts of categorisations of functional equations and I won't be getting into this for the sake of keeping it simple, but I hope you're starting to get a picture of what I'm saying. The **indeterminate (0/0)** and the **infinite (∞)** to go with the obvious, serve the purpose of the things in life that are currently undefined or too big a concept to wrap our heads around. (E.g. Do aliens exist? How many civilisations are out there? What does the Goddess look like?)

If you have a functional equation like, $(x^2 - 1)/(x - 1)$, although you're thinking it has no other variables so must be easy to solve, you'll find that when the **x** value is **1** (i.e. **x=1**) where $(1^2 - 1)/(1 - 1)= 0/0$ (the solution is indeterminate (unknown)). You were probably taught in high school that $(0/0 = 0)$ it's not, you were taught that for simplicity. Since the numerical value for 0/0 is unknown and has no defined value, we can find all the (**x**) values between 0 and 1 (**LHS**) to approach the answer (0/0) when **x=1** in Table 1. Look at the Cartesian scale in Figure 4 for further clarification.

Table 1

X (LHS)	$(x^2 - 1)/(x - 1)$
0.5	1.5
0.9	1.90
0.99	1.990

We can see from the table that as the **x** value gets closer to 1, the solution of the equation gets closer to 2. We use the word limit to say that as x approaches 1, the limit of $(x^2 - 1)/(x - 1)$ is therefore 2. This is represented as below:

$$\lim_{x \to 1} \frac{x^2 - 1}{x - 1} = 2$$

To be sure that the answer approaches 2, we can test the equation from the other side (**RHS**) of the (**x = 1**) values too. That is when x = 1.5, 1.1 and 1.01 in Table 2.

Table 2

X (RHS)	$(x^2 - 1)/(x - 1)$
1.5	2.5
1.1	2.10
1.01	2.010

Figure 4

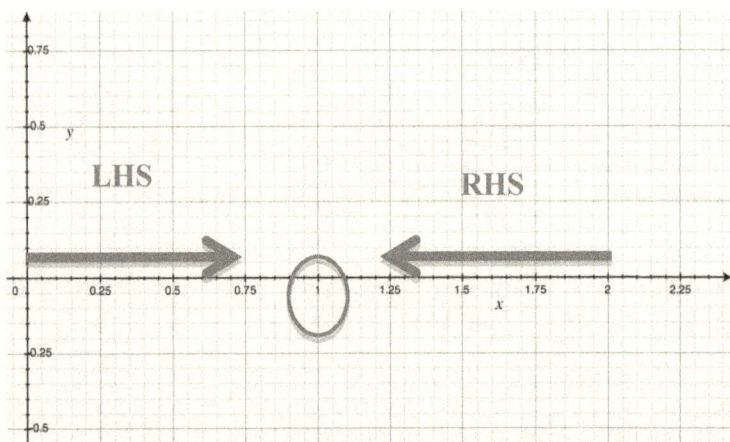

When approached from the left hand side of the (**x**) values, we get solutions of 1.5, 1.90, 1.990, and 1.9999 and so on. From the right we get solutions of 2.5, 2.10, and 2.010, therefore we are sure that the limit of this functional equation is 2.

A human life experience is as complex as functional equations. There are simply too many variables involved to reduce it to a simple algebraic equation. There are some aspects of our being that will remain indeterminate and other aspects that are infinite, but we can certainly try and find solution to our challenges by trial and error and get relatively close to what certain experiences might look and feel like given some known variables.

When we start to apply limits to daily life, you discover that they help us understand what it means to get arbitrarily close to a point, test the boundaries or acknowledge when something is unknown or infinite in nature. They are signs to let you know where you're going, what you may be getting yourself into and how far you can push the boundaries.

From another perspective, limits are also relative. They vary depending on the individual, beliefs and theme of exploration. If calculus is your thing and you're a bona fide maths geek, this equation is very easy to solve. If you have no interest in calculus and thus limited by knowledge you might find this equation difficult to unravel. Once you have the right knowledge and understanding at your fingertips to solve this equation it no longer becomes an impossible feat. Your awareness becomes a light that dispels the illusion of difficulty the mind created. The limits experienced by the mathematician and those experienced by the layperson are two different arbitrary points, based on the information and understanding they possess and nothing else. Your self-imposed limits may not actually be limits at all, once you shine the light of understanding and knowledge on it. By the way, I just wanted you to see how smart I was, there's absolutely no point here with these equations LOL.

By nature, and physicality, the human shell and what we know of it so far is also quite elementary. It's not so much that the human body is limited; it is our understanding, awareness and knowledge of it that needs major expansion. Generally, we are all bound by our mass ignorance, otherwise some of us will be flying around, and reading minds like the mutants portrayed in Marvel's X-Men. Humans are simply not at the stage of evolution yet, and whether we'll even evolve to resemble anything from Marvel is debatable. Science has always played catch up to our intuitive knowledge instead of working side by side with our body consciousness. Our cells have memory and knowledge we still haven't been able to tap into as a species, because some aspects of our scientific approach are resistant to intuition and the conscious Universe. If you go back to **Law of Vibration**, I touched lightly on L-Energy in The Heart's Code. The book by Pearson expands on what some scientists have found out concerning the heart and cell memory from transplant patients. There are reports of people who have certain knowledge at their fingertips after a transplant that was not there initially. How do we explain that?

I saw a video on YouTube the other day where some researchers have found that water has its own consciousness and responds to words and sound vibrations (remember everything vibrates). I haven't tried this out myself so I can't verify it, but a scientist in Japan Dr. Masaru Emoto, exposed water to different genres of music and words and documented the crystallised water structures. Water exposed to soothing music and positive words had beautifully formed symmetrical crystals whilst water crystals exposed to negative words or loud complex music structures were deformed and distorted. The video is labelled 'Water, Consciousness & Intent on

YouTube. Check it out for yourself. There are so many exciting things going on out there that the media refuses to expose us to. I brought up the water research because up to 65% of the human body is water, the brain 70%, lungs roughly 90% and around 80% of our blood is water. The Earth is mostly water too. Salt-water makes up 71% of the Earth's surface and 29% consists of continents and islands not counting the fresh water lakes, springs and tributaries. Think what we can achieve with our bodies and the planet with a lot of resources pumped into water, consciousness and intent research?

Some rules nonetheless can't be broken but can be overridden depending on your conscious toolkit and your level of awareness. There are some individuals who have apparently managed to override the collective mind script and manifested some unfathomable things; however, I suspect they are just more mindful of their full human potential and intelligence. I find that these folks are usually hermits for their own reasons, mainly to safeguard their knowledge and lifestyle from ignorance and ridicule. Humanity has always severely punished or misinterpreted the message of those who dared to live and think outside the norm, be it Jesus, Buddha, Muhammad and those who we have canonised and demonised throughout time.

In my opinion, the only reason we've had an explosion of knowledge and technology in the 19th and 20th century is because we went through an age of enlightenment (a collective awareness expansion), where some gave their lives willingly to carry on the legacy of mankind. Whichever way you look at it; the awful past was necessary to give us this present moment. Because of our set up, every chosen theme and purpose on Earth has a shelf life of time. The limit of time is also imposed on us because we filter our experiences in doses. Time is divided in seconds, minutes, hours, days, weeks, months and years because it makes it more bite size. This thankfully provides closure to the highs and lows of human experience. If you miss out on something the infinite Universe will ensure it is handled in this life or the next since we have all of eternity.

The Earth also has its own consciousness because it is a living, breathing organism and is self-regulated. Mother Nature has certain agreed upon parameters, for all those who wish to inhabit planet Earth. There's gravity, three laws of motion, conservation of mass energy, laws of thermodynamics, conservation, electrostatic laws, speed of light and Einstein's theory of relativity amongst others. Abusing the planet, we inhabit has its very own cause and effects. It's imperative to get Gaia's blessing, whatever we choose to do on this planet because then everything works and comes together perfectly and harmoniously. Now I know what you're thinking; Pocahontas was right all along (Disney's Colours of The Wind is my joint). This isn't to say that the West has it all wrong with the concrete jungle way of life; it's just one way out of an immeasurable number that we can choose to experience physical reality. Conscious living and sustainability takes on many forms and I can see a rise in our awareness in the UK with the rise of things like recycling, upcycling, corporate social responsibility and eco-friendly building projects.

Why Earth? Well why not? Earth is a matrix, a chessboard of sorts and as spiritual beings, a vital part of our consciousness is plugged into this reality and parts of it are in other realities or dimensions. Quite frankly this planet is pretty primitive in nature. The primitive aspect is probably what drives us here and explains why there are over 7 billion of us. I like to think we come here just for the sheer pleasure of it. We journey into this sphere, with the purpose of investigating physical life and its potential. Each experience is only one of its kind on a higher level. Our natural unique energy is constantly expanding, learning, tuning in, and sorting through it for the exhilaration of it all, because joy, excitement and transformation is the point of all of it. Life is all about the business of adding value and this is done through experience.

You willingly come here, because you know your soul will always keep an eye on you and keep its ear to broader perspective whilst you're plugged into physical reality. Just as you can multi-task in your daily life your overall soul **(Oversoul)** is focused on many different incarnations at once. The **Oversoul** is sometimes referred to as the Higher Self and it is tasked with the job of managing your affairs, whilst you maintain a level of free will because ultimately you always have the final choice. Some people call the Oversoul your guardian angel or lately your guidance angel. The better your understanding of life and how it works, the more aligned you are with your Oversoul and the natural laws of life. Jane Robert's Oversoul Seven Trilogy although fictional, does an excellent job in painting the idea of an Oversoul.

Not only do we project our fear based egotistic agenda on human purpose and existence, we also project these warped ideas on our level of intelligence too. We have a brain with over one hundred billion cells and connections and yet we limit intelligence to an IQ test? Theorists believe that there are nine types of intelligence, yet we seem to only hone in on a couple and filter all our experiences through it. Those who believe in the two-dimensional form of intelligence, typically linguistic and logical-mathematical reasoning alone throw out knowledge that comes instinctively and intuitively with no full grounding or empirical research. The human brain is what sets us apart from other conscious life forms on the planet and you want to reduce it to mathematics and language? The accepted forms of knowledge have forced us to focus purely in a linear time-space manner and discard other sensory intuitive data. There are certain things I can pick up from one single interaction with someone, which from the outside looking in will render presumptuous. Any concept outside of the accepted framework is labelled 'quack' and ultimately becomes alien to our human and cultural upbringing. As Henry Ford said *'thinking is the hardest job there is, that is why so few people engage in it'*.

We are equipped with an all-knowing intuitive heart and a body consciousness; tune it to the frequency of unconditional love and listen to it. Some of the things that resonate with us cannot be expressed linguistically or proved empirically yet. This is human conditioning at its best. Remember that science plays catch up to human abilities. **It is not until it happens are we able to scientifically document it.**

In his book *Frames of Mind: The Theory of Multiple Intelligences*, Howard Gardner suggests that intelligence can be categorised into three things:

1) The ability to create an effective product or offer a service that is valued in a culture,

2) A set of skills that make it possible for a person to solve problems in life, and

3) The potential for finding or creating solutions for problems, which involves gathering new knowledge.

When you break these down further you get nine classifications of intelligence. I've summarised them below. For more information either purchase his book or peruse the net (Nine Classifications of Intelligence) for a summary of his work.

According to Gardner the nine classifications are:

- **Naturalist Intelligence** ('Nature Smart'),

  - Sensitivity to and conscious awareness of all
    life forms in the natural world. This individual
    is said to have extra-sensory perception.

- **Musical Intelligence** ('Musical Smart'),

  - The ability to discern pitch, rhythm, timbre, and
    tone. Some individuals can hear a song once and
    play it perfectly. There is said to be a connection
    between music and e-motion (energy in motion).

- **Logical-Mathematical Intelligence**
  ('Number/Reasoning Smart'),

  - This is the ability to calculate, quantify,
    consider propositions and hypotheses, and
    carry out complete mathematical operations.

- **Existential Intelligence** (Cosmic Smart),

  - Sensitivity and capacity to tackle deep
    questions about human existence, such as the
    meaning of life, why we die, and how we got
    here? (I reckon this is more my forte, my

domain, my 'queendom'. I am joking of course).

- **Interpersonal Intelligence** (People Smart"),

  o The knack to understand and interact effectively with others. It involves effective verbal and nonverbal communication.

- **Bodily-Kinaesthetic Intelligence** ("Body Smart"),

  o The gift to manipulate objects and use a variety of physical skills. This intelligence also involves a sense of timing and the perfection of skills through mind–body union.

- **Linguistic Intelligence** (Word Smart),

  o The ability to think in words and use language to express and appreciate complex meanings. Wordsmith also comes to mind.

- **Intra-personal Intelligence** ("Self Smart"),

  o The capacity to understand oneself and one's thoughts and feelings. Possessing a depth of attention and awareness that enables you to focus and make flexible life plans.

- **Spatial Intelligence** ("Picture Smart")

o Spatial intelligence is the ability to reason in three dimensions. Core capacities include mental imagery, spatial reasoning, image manipulation, graphic and artistic skills, and an active imagination.

I love Gardner's classifications because I think they encompass all the permutations of human intelligence. However, all forms of intelligence are grounded in attention and awareness. If you're focused enough on anything, giving it 100% of your energy, you will open up your body consciousness to it and absorb all it has to offer. On the other hand, you can argue that because this is already innate in us, by going through the motions and the gazillion processes we buy into we are able to become more of who we naturally are: GENIUSES! Remember, processes don't define us we give it meaning. The source of attention and awareness is consciousness itself. Our human learning, history and conditioning has trained us out of this knowledge.

Remaining open to intra-personal and existential intelligence is of great importance, if we are to survive and unite as humanity as the foundation of a fulfilled life starts with knowing yourself and your value. Re-discovering your God/Goddess nature is one of the most important phases of human development or dare I say it only career worth pursuing. No material possession, job, lifestyle is more valuable than connecting to your higher, instinctive, innovative, self, the big YOU and understanding your individual right to a great, fun-filled adventurous life. Remember that YOU are the fabric and essence of God personified, accept it because you are made in the likeness and the heart of the Creator.

All of the nine classifications are inherent in all of us, some in varying degrees than others depending on our chosen theme and purpose. A vast majority of us hardly spend time really thinking about who we are and our purpose for existence. Until we have some unified answers as to why we are here and what we're doing, we'll forever be waging wars, exploiting and manipulating each other with various agendas. It's time to get off autopilot and question our societal structure. Poke around and decide for yourselves what kind of reality you prefer to live in.

If you've bought into the idea of an infinite expansive Universe, then you'll also be inclined to think humans limit the universal energy by assuming they are the only intelligent life forms inhabiting this vast space. In the slightly paraphrased words of Prof. Brian Cox in The Human Universe, *'It has taken us 200,000 years to transform the ape-man into a space-man'*. Now that alone is an achievement in itself. If you're on the leading edge, you're probably backing space exploration, because the world of space exploration is a way to take humanity into the cosmos. Space gives us more insight into our origins as humans. Besides the last thing we want is to be caught unaware of intergalactic happenings. To put it into perspective in The

Hitchhiker's Guide to the Galaxy, Arthur Dent wakes up to find that his house is being destroyed by the council to make way for a bypass. Meanwhile his friend Ford Prefect an extra-terrestrial from Betelgeuse, stranded on Earth for fifteen years is about to deliver the news about Earth's seemingly sudden destruction by the Vogons to make way for a hyperspatial express route through the Earth's star system.

When you go on to read it, if you haven't already, which by the way I highly recommend, you'll find out that the council pre-warned Arthur about their bypass, just as the Galactic Hyperspace Planning council pre-warned Earth about the express route though they had no way of knowing about it because they never paid attention to anything else but life on earth. Like many other planets and galaxies, they thought they were the only ones in the Universe. The book is a light-hearted fictional comedy, but juxtaposed with Arthur's immediate concerns of being homeless (humanity's pressing needs about bills, money, religion (whose God and bank balance is bigger?) coupled with Earth's demolition tells you there's always a bigger picture going on that one needs to be aware of atheist or not. We've obviously come a long way since Douglas Adams wrote The Hitchhiker...

Essentially, I'm gunning for a seat on the Virgin Galactic or any other commercial flight journeying into space as I've always wanted to be an astronaut without having to study for it. I'm really not that fussed as long as we go and I hear David Bowie's Space Oddity mid-flight and there is a Major Tom in ground control.

In a Nutshell...

- There are no limits bar the ones you have imposed on yourself.
- Limits are choices and a life without them is quite frankly quite dull one.
- With knowledge and awareness, self-imposed limits will no longer prove necessary.
- We need more research into water, consciousness and intent (when I win the Euro Millions I might just fund this myself).
- The Earth is an awesome place to learn about creativity.
- Surely we can't be the only intelligent life forms in this vast space?

"This business of deliberate Creation can be turned into an engineering feat, but the true power of your experience lies in the silence between the words, the vibrational rhythm between the thoughts, the ease between the effort and the peace between the trying. The true power is in allowing the universe to yield to you what you have already queued up for it. So think as long as it's fun, try as long it's easy, speak as long as it feels good and otherwise take a nap."

Esther Hicks

FINAL THOUGHTS

When I finally understood the depth of all the material covered in this book, I couldn't wait to create and master a better life for myself. You cannot talk about the human experience without factoring in the spiritual purpose for existence. It took me at least a couple of years to wrap my head around most of it. Some of the things I've mentioned will reveal themselves to you in the middle of a challenge, whilst some will prove very easy to comprehend. Each decision I made subsequently always lead me right back to self-discovery. Everyone and everything took on a new identity of teacher and nurturer. Nothing offended me anymore, because everything was there to teach me to love all of me. I find that when people awaken or become enlightened, in their attempt and excitement to teach they invalidate all other experiences and proclaim their path to be the only and most righteous way. It isn't about right or wrong but rather what you want out of life. I believe there are many roads to fulfilment, happiness and enlightenment, which is essentially what life is about. As they say 'variety is the spice of life' and if there was only one path, there would only be one person.

Here's what I suggest you can do for yourself in no particular order:

1. Remember that you create your own reality.

2. Be your natural self, as best you can from moment-to-moment.

3. Put stock into yourself instead of an arbitrary system. It's the only thing guaranteed to go up in value indefinitely.

4. What is acceptable for one is not acceptable for another. One size does not fit all. In my opinion, it doesn't matter how you find the life force as long as you find it.

5. To remove negative beliefs and stereotypes, get rid of the supporting data and watch those beliefs crumble.

6. Lighten up and laugh more, as this is all an illusion and nothing is perfect. It's designed that way to keep you reaching for more.

7. Commit to one thing every couple of months. Because everything is linked and all are one, any situation can actually affect all areas of your life.

8. Wake up every day and be grateful for your family, friends, home, and health. Find something, anything to be content with.

9. Reframe everything to your advantage using the emotional scale. The best life is the one you currently know and have, think any different and you're on a slippery slope.

10. Enjoy and celebrate your growth with those who are on the same journey as you.

11. Remain open to all things and don't shove your newfound light unto others. That creates unnecessary resistance. Trust that life will teach them, just like it taught you.

12. There are countless books; unlimited counsel and the Internet embrace it. Don't take my word for anything I write about, I mean what the hell do I know? Find out for yourself. In the words of my other BFF Albert Einstein, *'Play is the highest form of research'*. There's really nothing too serious going on here.

13. Question anything that is divisive to the collective human agenda. Anything that causes tension and segregation definitely needs both eyebrows raised.

14. You are worthy and awesome and I appreciate you beyond words.

15. If it's a sure thing, why rush?

ACKNOWLEDGMENTS

My darling mother thanks for having complete blind faith in me.

Nuru Adam, I couldn't have asked for a better and more honest second support system.

Madalina Paval, you were the first person I told about writing this book. Thank you for being that soft place to land and for always thinking of me.

I am indebted to those who took the time out to read my drafts: Neelum Yousaf (my nelly minelly) and Cynthia Appenteng (mother and wife of the year). Without your energetic input, intelligence and exceptional generosity, it would have been a completely different book.

I am grateful to Amanda Osei-Agyemang, Noelle Osei-Agyemang and Samuel Appenteng, the Adam family, Pietro (GG) and Elizabeth Marini for feeding me waakye, jollof, fufu, lamb chops, roast chicken, fish, fried yam, iftar, scallops, tiramisu, providing me with WiFi, countless sleepovers, laughter and many random conversations. Thank you playing with me, pushing me, distracting me, caring for me, feeding me, creating with me and having fun with me. My fun-employed quest would have been desert-dry without you.

Palak Bhatt (bhatt cheeks), that trek up to Nevis proved useful seeing as it gave me such a beautiful backdrop to my website and a bloody sore left knee.

For the unwavering support of these dear ones, who played a part in the process one way or another, I am truly grateful; Daniel Darko, Kojo Gambrah-Sampaney, Kodjo Boama, Javada Appenteng, Madalina Paval, Edwina Knight, Alicja Worytiewic, , Alberto Dallalonga, Hardeep Kooner (hakuna Matata), Naseeka (nasminder) Busawon, Livy Sache, Amera Otaifa, Deborah Defoe, Eki Izevbigie, Angel Agyei-Ampadu, Nnamdi Efobi, Alexandra Seeboruth, Rebecca Bianchi, Yuka Aoki, Peter Quarshie, Shakerul Haque, Jerry Appenteng Darac. Thank you also for user testing my website and putting up with my incessant Whatsapp harassments and shameless plugs.

To the extended family, including family friends, you have all played a part in my journey. By being you, I was able to be myself with little to zero resistance. Thank you.

To those speakers and writers who inspired me in more ways than they could ever imagine; the late Dr Myles Munroe, Esther Hicks, Darryl Anka, Jane Roberts, Paulo Coehlo (Warrior Of The Light), Tony Robbins, Peter J. Daniels, Pat Mesiti and Brian Tracy, Jim Rohn, thank you. Although I don't subscribe to or agree with everything they say some of their words have rung true for me.

Swiss Post Solutions at Bupa House, what would I do without your ring binding expertise?

Shout out to 'clker.com' for the outline of my three-legged stool.

A special shout out to the British Library and the Edmonton Green Library for giving me a safe place to work.

To the wonderful world of self-publishing, thank you so much for a steep but sharp learning curve. The dream always costs more than you budget for.

And finally to Neil Taylor, 'Le Feebs' wouldn't be *Le Feebs* without your sharp-witted tongue, thank you.

The list is endless, for the sake of brevity I will end here.

FURTHER READING

My reading list is never ending but this is a snapshot of some of the books on Kindle and iBooks. It's extremely varied, open and fun. I know I've learned something from some or all of these books though I can't quite remember exactly what from some of them (LOL). I have books on my e-shelf I haven't made time for yet, maybe in another life since I have all of eternity. If you were expecting to see the classics, sorry to disappoint but I'd much rather watch them in a series or a film with subtitles on. I hear it's the same as reading it.

- The Alchemist - Paulo Coehlo

  What's not to love about the boy Santiago who dared to follow his dreams?

- The Wind in the Willows - Kenneth Grahame

  Everyone needs a mole, a badger and toad in their lives.

- Anatomy of Peace - Arbinger Institute

  Interesting short story on how one can solve conflict with a peaceful heart.

- The Oversoul 7: Trilogy - Jane Roberts

  A fictional depiction on how our Oversoul keeps an eye on its various incarnations. I found it simply scrumptious to read.

- Bared to You Series - Sylvia Day

  A little something to keep a girl energised, during the fun single times.

- Mr. Unavailable and the Fallback Girl - Natalie Lue

  If you can't seem to attract that wonderful guy and have no idea why, I urge you to read this book.

- 50 Shades of Grey Trilogy - E.L. James

  Refer to Bared to You.

- Purple Hibiscus - Chimamanda Ngozi Adichie

  A very vivid fictional narrative about the blurred lines between love and hate, the journey into adulthood and the lines between the ancestral gods and the western gods set in Nigeria. If you loved Things Fall Apart by Chinua Achebe, you will undoubtedly love this.

- Ask & It is Given - Esther & Jerry Hicks

  Abraham who Esther channels is very soothing and reassuring. It's a little bit more background information into the law of attraction and the workings of the Universe.

- Career Helium - David Thompson

  I just fell in love with it when I read. If you're in the corporate world and feel a little lost on how to advance, I recommend.

- The Game of Life and How to Play It - Florence Scovel-Shinn

  This book requires you to exercise total faith in everything to the point that it's transformed into certainty.

- Seth - Jane Roberts

  Seth is a higher consciousness that Jane channels and who I have to thank for a chunk of the information in here. He blows my mind every time.

- Way of The Peaceful Warrior - Dan Millman

  A guy I was seeing recommended this book and thank God he did.

- A Woman of Substance - Barbara Taylor Bradford

  Emma Harte is a woman after my own heart. It's a gripping tale of a woman who goes from a kitchen maid to the most respected woman in business. She creates a better life for herself with her choices.

- The Hitchhiker's Guide To The Galaxy - Douglas Adams

  Pure Genius! Recommended by the same guy who suggested I read Way Of The Peaceful Warrior.

- And They Were Not Ashamed - Laura M. Brotherson

  An informative book about women's sexual conditioning and inhibitions. It's a fascinating read if you can look past the religious rigmarole.

- The Bible & Other Religious Books – Moses et al

  It's man's imagination at its best and I am not an atheist. There are some wonderful insights in there, just look past the obvious contradictions and don't bother highlighting it too.

SOME OF MY FAVOURITE QUOTES

- "I have no special talents. I am only passionately curious. "-Albert Einstein
- "A person's a person, no matter how small."- Dr Seuss
- "It's our choices Harry that show us who we truly are, far more than our abilities."- Albus Dumbledore
- "Whatever your past has been, you have a spotless future."- Melanie Gustafson
- "People often say that motivation doesn't last. Well, neither does bathing- that's why we recommend it daily."- Zig Ziglar
- Piglet: "How do you spell love?"
  Pooh: "You don't spell it, you feel it." – A.A. Milne
- "For a man to conquer himself is the first and noblest of all victories."- Plato
- "It's not just about living forever Jackie, the trick is living with yourself forever."- Pirates of the Caribbean.

- "A human being is part of the whole called by us universe, a part limited in time and space. He experiences himself, his thoughts and feelings as something from the rest, a kind of optical delusion of his consciousness. This delusion is a kind of prison for us, restricting us to our personal desires for a few persons nearest to us. Our task is to free ourselves from this prison by widening the circle of compassion to embrace all living creatures and the whole of nature in its beauty."- Albert Einstein.

THANK YOU

Like all great adventures, mine began with a moment of insanity, an urge to quit a decent city job and I listened to it. I am eternally grateful that you took the time out to read, consider and explore what I have to say. You are so generous and totally amaze-balls. Perhaps I've ruffled a few feathers, perhaps I haven't but as it's my first book, do go easy on the review, as I don't intend to be a one-book wonder. On a spice scale I hope I've blown your mind to 150,000 scoville units, ok maybe 30,000 units instead. The fundamental ideas expressed here are nothing new or at least I think they're old. The gist of what I have to say is scattered all over the World Wide Web, countless books, blogs, channelers and studies.

This is a brief account of my journey so far and in my opinion some undeniable insights into life. I'd love to hear from you with any questions, concerns or comments regarding this book, or even my website. Did I overlook something? Have you developed your own life strategies you would like to share? Or simply want to chat? Please get in touch. I'm always tickled pink when I read the comment section of any article, so if you can't leave a nice comment please be creative and hilarious. Feel free to contact me at www.lefeebs.com or alternately find me on Twitter '@lefeebs', Facebook: www.facebook.com/lefeebsofficial or Instagram: lefeebsofficial

CHEERS!

www.ingramcontent.com/pod-product-compliance
Lightning Source LLC
LaVergne TN
LVHW011158080426
835508LV00007B/468